THE OFFICIAL®

Price Guide to

AMERICAN
PATRIOTIC
MEMORABILIA

WITHDRAWN

THE OFFICIAL®
Price Guide to
AMERICAN
PATRIOTIC
MEMORABILIA

Michael Polak

HOUSE OF COLLECTIBLES
NEW YORK

Important Notice: All of the information, including valuations, in this book has been compiled from the most reliable sources, and every effort has been made to eliminate errors and questionable data. Nevertheless, the possibility of error, in a work of such scope, always exists. The publisher will not be held responsible for losses that may occur in the purchase, sale, or other transaction of items because of information contained herein. Readers who feel they have discovered errors are invited to *write* and inform us, so they may be corrected in subsequent editions. Those seeking further information on the topics covered in this book are advised to refer to the complete line of *Official Price Guides* published by the House of Collectibles.

HOUSE OF
COLLECTIBLES
House of Collectibles is a registered trademark and the colophon is a trademark of Random House, Inc.

Published by House of Collectibles
Random House Reference
New York, NY

Distributed by Random House Reference, a division of Random House Inc., New York, and simultaneously in Canada by Random House of Canada Limited, Toronto.

www.houseofcollectibles.com

Printed in the United States of America

ISBN 0-609-81014-6

10 9 8 7 6 5 4 3 2 1

First Edition

Contents

Dedication

This first edition of *American Patriotic Memorabilia* is dedicated to those men and women of the United States Military who have made the ultimate sacrifice in the war on terrorism, along with the families of these brave men and women. Also, to the brave men and women proudly serving in the U.S. military who continue to put themselves in harm's way on a daily basis in the battle to win the war on terrorism.

Your mission is one of honor and courage, and you are to be commended.

THANK YOU.

Acknowledgments

When I began gathering information to write *American Patriotic Memorabilia*, I knew that despite my passion for patriotism I was going to need additional help from collectors, dealers, and experts knowledgeable in the history of America and its patriotic memorabilia. Along the way, I formed some great friendships that I hope will last well into the future. All of these great individuals provided much needed help and expertise. I would like to say "Thank you" to the following special people who provided much needed help and expertise:

Gerald E. Czulewicz, Sr. (the real Mr. Uncle Sam)

Diana Douglas and Michael J. Ogle, American Garage (Folk Art)

Ira and Larry Goldberg Coins and Collectibles

Hallmark Cards

Howard Hazelcorn

Bruce Hershenson

Sandra Hollman

Martin Jacobs (World War II Homefront Collectibles)

James D. Julia, Inc. Auctions

Peter Gwillim Kreitler (*United We Stand*)

Michael Laurence, Scott Publishing Company

Sandy Marrone

Bill Retskin

Paul Riseman

Sayles Graphic Design ("Art Fights Back")

Martin Shapiro (Vintage Postcards)

Steve Slotin, Slotin Folk Art Auctions

Sotheby's Auctions

Meyda Tiffany Company

Betsy Towle (Postal History Foundation)

Doug Watson (Paper Collectors Marketplace)

Lynn Wenzel

Photo Credits

Diana Douglas and Michael J. Ogle, American Garage (Folk Art)

Ira and Larry Goldberg Coins and Collectibles

Hallmark Cards, Inc.

Howard Hazelcorn

Sandra Hollman

Martin Jacobs

James D. Julia, Inc. Auctions

Peter Gwillim Kreitler

Michael Laurence, Scott Publishing Company

Bill Retskin

Paul Riseman

Sayles Graphic Design

Martin Shapiro

Steve Slotin, Slotin Folk Art Auctions

Sotheby's

Meyda Tiffany Company

Lynn Wenzel

Introduction

*W*elcome to the first edition of *American Patriotic Memorabilia* and the fun hobby of collecting patriotic memorabilia and collectibles. Patriotism is defined as "love of country, public spirit, good citizenship, and national-ism," and there's never been a doubt that "love of country" has been the core motto of our country, even before the signing of the Declaration of Independence. Since the tragic events of September 11, 2001, patriotism in the United States has evoked a much stronger and more emotional awareness of "love of country." While writing this book, I wanted to capture our strong passion of patriotism by presenting the many types of memorabilia that have been reflective of the United States since its beginning.

In order to make *American Patriotic Memorabilia* the best and most informative reference and pricing guide available, I have provided a broad range of detailed infor-mation useful to both the beginner and the veteran collector. I have included a broad range of chapters, covering such topics as the history of patriotic memorabilia and on memorabilia sources to assist in the understanding and locating of special treasures and finds. Other chapters pertain to flags, Uncle Sam, stamps, and political and military items. Also featured are about 150 photographs and detailed pricing to aid collectors in understanding the hobby and identifying their collections. The dollar values attached to the listings indicate the value of that particular piece based on current information and input from dealers, collectors, and various auction houses and will provide a good starting point for pricing items in your collection or items that you are considering as additions. For reference and research purposes, I have included detailed chapters on collectors, clubs and associations, dealers, recommended books and periodicals, mu-seum and research resources, and auction houses and services.

While collecting patriotic memorabilia can be a very profitable venture, I believe that most collectors look beyond the value of the item and into its origin and history. In fact, I find that researching the item itself can prove to be more interesting than the search for the item. I enjoy both pursuits for their close ties to the rich history of the settling of the United States and their impact on the patriotism that has never left our country. I hope that the first edition of *American Patriotic Memorabilia* will provide you not only with an increased understanding and enjoyment of the hobby of collecting patriotic memorabilia but also a strong reinforcement and renewed passion of patriotism and love of our country, the United States of America.

Patriotism in America

I can't begin to say enough about the patriotism of Americans and their love of this country. I'm sure that when I was born, someone put a U.S. flag in my hands and I've never let go. Patriotism has always been the strong and moving force behind America that has propelled—and continues to propel—this great nation to answer the bell during the most tragic events and moments of history. Moments in time such as World Wars I and II, Korea, Vietnam, the Gulf War, and now, the tragic events of September 11, 2001.

Since September 2001, this country has demonstrated its patriotic passion, giving a message to the world that America is great and will not be divided by terrorists or anyone else trying to bring harm to its citizens. I knew this strong passion existed, but until I began to gather information for this book and talked with many people in the process, I really didn't realize the depth of that patriotism. I'd like to share some of the things that Americans have been doing to demonstrate their patriotism in answer to this recent defining moment in American history.

As usual, America could depend on its government to immediately take action. Shortly after September 11, several U.S. senators and congressmen sent a letter to Treasury Secretary Paul O'Neill, urging the issuance of patriotic bonds to help pay for the fight against terrorism and the continuing relief efforts. Soon thereafter, the Treasury Department announced that it would be issuing war bonds, the first such issuance since World War II. The U.S. government has issued war bonds to help with the financing of war efforts beginning with the Revolutionary War and continuing through World Wars I and II. In December 2001, the U.S. government issued the Series EE Savings Bonds with the inscription "Patriotic Bond." In keeping with the strong message of patriotism, a new 34¢ stamp was unveiled on October 2, 2001, featuring a fluttering American flag with the words "United We Stand" along the bottom of the border.

This surge in patriotism was continued by the business and private sectors through various events. As America entered the 2001 holiday season, with the country in conflict and war, Hallmark Cards issued four new patriotic greeting cards using traditional holiday images. These cards sent messages of peace, hope, and patriotism with images depicting wreaths and snowmen wrapped in red, white, and blue, waving the American flag. As a continued expression of patriotism, many artists and manufacturers of contemporary collectibles joined in the effort by designing unique patriotic pieces and donating the proceeds from sales to various relief organizations. One of the most moving and inspirational items that expressed America's emotion and patriotism is a Cottage Garden print by D. Morgan titled "We Are the Eagles in the Storm." This piece depicts an American eagle overlooking three firemen raising the American flag against a backdrop of a larger American flag. Other items with portions of the donations benefiting various relief organizations were "Brave Heart," a Christopher Radko ornament from the "Christmas Glories Collection"; "Stars 'n' Stripes," a paperweight from Caithness Glass; "Long May It Wave," a Dreamsicles figurine from Cast Art; "When I Grow Up Firefighter" and "I Love America," dolls from Lee Middleton Original Dolls; and "Fireman," a Royal Doulton figurine.

One of the most striking displays of patriotism centered around an exhibit by the Smithsonian National Museum of American History called "July 1942: United We Stand," which ran through October 2002. As America was entering World War II, approximately 500 magazines embarked on an ambitious campaign to inspire the nation by featuring an American flag on their covers for the Fourth of July 1942 issue. Along with the depiction of the flag, approximately half of the magazines included the slogan "United We Stand." While the "Magazines" chapter in this book lists and depicts a number of these magazine covers, the recently published book titled *United We Stand,* by Peter Gwillim Kreitler, features more than 100 of these covers. The Smithsonian exhibit provides the American public with a unique opportunity to view this special page in history, while at the same time supporting the nation with its current surge in patriotism.

In unprecedented numbers, Americans want to show their patriotism and love of country. On September 15, 2001, local sponsors planned on 6,000 residents to form a living flag with a picture being taken from the air in order to make postcards. The postcards were then given to those who donated to a fund for victims in New York, and additional cards were sold for 50¢ each. As a true show of patriotism, an additional 9,000 people showed up. These extras were worked into the living flag, making a grand total of 15,000. And on May 23, 2002, Sotheby's conducted an auction of rare American flags dating back to the pre-Revolutionary War flag. This flag is the only known example of its type, with 13 red and white stripes and the blue star field being replaced by a Union Jack, which was the symbol of the British flag. The flag brought a price of $163,500, which was a world record for an American flag at an auction. In all, 80 flags brought in a total dollar amount of $1.3 million. According to Dr. Jeffery Kohn, Sotheby's consultant to the auction, "Less than four flags out of 80 went to flag collectors . . . the rest went to Americana collectors or people who are new to collecting." He went on to say, "This is another patriotic surge, which gets us all to look at our roots and meanings of objects. . . . We're talking about freedom, and it's embodied in a flag."

But not just a flag—it's our flag. The flag of every American. Keep it up, America— never let our patriotism die.

Patriotic Memorabilia Sources

*P*atriotic memorabilia collectibles, antique or current items, can be found in a variety of locations, sometimes where you least expect them. I think that the search, or hunt for that hard-to-find item, is as much fun as finding the item. The following sources are good potential hiding places for that much sought-after patriotic item and will help with your search for that special find.

The Internet

In the 30 years that I've been collecting, I've never seen anything impact the world of collecting as much as the Internet. Since the tragedy of September 11, 2001, patriotism has never been stronger, and the Internet has experienced a growth in patriotic memorabilia that will most likely never be matched again with any collectible item. Simply log on to the Internet, type in "patriotic memorabilia," and you'll be amazed with the amount of data that will appear at your fingertips.

There are numerous Web sites throughout the United States, Canada, and Europe that provide information about clubs, dealers, antique publications, and auction companies. These sites have literally opened up the entire world to the collector and have become the best, most inexpensive, and most valuable resources for the collector and the dealer alike.

Flea Markets, Swap Meets, Thrift and Secondhand Stores, Garage Sales, Salvage Stores

For the beginner collector, these sources will likely be the most fun and yield the most items at the best prices. As discussed earlier, a little bit of homework and research can result in opportunities to purchase an endless variety of patriotic items for an extremely low cost. When you are searching flea markets, swap meets, and thrift stores, be sure to target those areas where the odds and ends are being sold. It's a good bet there will be some type of patriotic items. When targeting garage sales, try to concentrate your search in the older areas of town since the items being presented for sale will be noticeably older, more collectible, and more likely to fall into a rare category. Salvage stores or salvage yards are great places to search since these businesses deal with companies that have contracts to demolish old houses, apartments, and businesses and on occasion will come across treasures.

Local Clubs and Collectors

By joining a local club with a focus on your specialty or by working with other collectors, you will find yet another source for your growing collection. Collectors will usually have quantities of unwanted or duplicate items, which they will sell very reasonably, trade, or sometimes simply give away, especially to an enthusiastic new collector. In addition, clubs are always a good source of information about other resources for the treasure hunter.

Antique Shows

Antique shows not only expose you to items of every type, shape, color, and variety but also provide you with the opportunity to talk with many experts in specialized fields. In addition, you will usually find publications for sale, or being given away, relating to all aspects of collecting the various items of patriotic memorabilia as referenced in this book. Antique shows can be a rewarding learning experience for the beginner collector in particular but also for the veteran collector; these shows take place almost every weekend all across the country. There is always something new to learn and share and, of course, items to buy or trade. One last note: Make sure you look under the tables at these shows since many bargains in the form of duplicates and unwanted items may be lurking where you least expect them.

Auction and Estate Sales

Auction houses have always been a good source of patriotic items. When looking for an auction, try to find an auction house that specializes in antiques and estate buyouts. To promote itself and provide buyers with a better idea of what will be presented for sale, an auction house usually publishes a catalog that provides descriptions, details on conditions, and photographs of items. Auctions are fun and can be a very good source at economical prices if you pay attention to what you are doing. I do recommend, however, that you visit an auction first as a spectator to learn a little about how the whole process works before you decide to participate and buy at one. When buying, be sure of the condition of the items as well as the terms of the sale. These guidelines also apply to all Internet auctions. Since buying and selling at auctions have become exceedingly popular, here are some general rules and information to consider:

Buying through Auctions

★ Purchase the catalog and review all the items in the auction. If you are attending a live auction, there is usually a preview prior to the auction in order for shoppers to actually see the items.

★ After reviewing the catalog and making your choice, you usually phone or mail in your bid. (A 10 percent buyer's premium is usually added to the sale price.)

★ Callbacks allow you to increase the previous high bid (including yours) on certain items after the close of the auction.

★ A bidder with the winning bid will have an invoice sent, and after the check clears, the item will be shipped.

★ The majority of auction houses have a return policy; if the item you purchased doesn't meet the description in the catalog, there is usually a refund policy.

At the end of this book, "Auction Houses and Services" lists a number of quality auction houses that specialize in categories outlined in this book.

Selling through Auctions

★ The first action to take is to check out your auction source before consigning over any merchandise. Make sure that the auction venue is legitimate and has not had any problems with payments or products.

★ After you decide on the auction house, package the item with plenty of bubble pack, insure your item, and then mail the package by certified mail, sign receipt requested.

★ Following the completion of the auction, you might have to wait up to 30 days to receive the check from the proceeds of the sale. The majority of firms will charge a 15 percent seller commission of the sales price.

Estate sales are great sources if the home is in a very old neighborhood or section of the city that has historical significance. These sales are a lot of fun, especially when the people running the sale let you look over and handle the items for sale, which will help you to make careful selections. Prices are usually good and are generally negotiable.

Knife and Gun Shows

What, patriotic items at a knife and gun show? Quite a number of gun and knife enthusiasts are also great fans of the West and rich in patriotism and often keep an eye open for related artifacts. Every knife and gun show I've attended, or sold at, has had numerous dealers with different types of patriotic items on (or under) their tables for sale. And the prices were about right since they were more interested in selling their knives and guns than the bottles or other items. Plus, these dealers will often provide information on where they made their finds, which you can put to good use later in tracking some down on your own.

Retail Antique Dealers

This grouping includes those dealers who sell items at or near full market prices. Buying from a dealer has its upside as well as its downside. Dealers usually have a large selection and will provide helpful information and details about the item you want. It is a safe bet that items for sale are authentic and have been priced in accordance with the true condition of the item.

On the other hand, trying to build up a collection by purchasing from these dealers can be very expensive. But these shops are a good place to browse, learn, and try and add to your collection.

General Antique and Specialty Shops

The main differences between a general shop and a retail dealer are that usually the selection is more limited with a general shop and the prices of most items are usually quite a bit lower. The variance in pricing is partly because dealers in a general shop are usually not as knowledgeable about the items being sold and therefore may incorrectly identify an item, overlooking critical areas that determine the value. If a collector can become knowledgeable, these general antique dealers can provide the opportunity to acquire quality underpriced merchandise.

The "Pledge of Allegiance"

I pledge allegiance to the Flag of the United States of America, and to the Republic for which it stands, one Nation under God, indivisible, with liberty and justice for all.

—*Current version of the "Pledge of Allegiance"*

A book about patriotic memorabilia wouldn't be complete without some words about our "Pledge of Allegiance" to the United States of America. And recently, quite a few words have been said about the pledge. A June 2002 ruling by California's Ninth Circuit Court of Appeals struck down a 1954 law passed by Congress that added "under God" to the pledge, affecting public schools in nine Western states. Needless to say, this ignited quite a controversy prior to the Fourth of July.

The following is the original "Pledge of Allegiance," as written by Baptist minister Francis Bellamy in 1892 for a family magazine:

I pledge allegiance to my Flag and the Republic for which it stands, one nation, indivisible, with liberty and justice for all.

This early version of the pledge was adopted by the first National Flag Conference held in Washington D.C., in 1923. Since a number of the individuals attending the conference were worried that the use of the words "my Flag" could create confusion for the numerous immigrants entering America, a decision was made to change the words to "the Flag of the United States of America." With the high surge of patriotism as American entered World War II, the "Pledge of Allegiance" was officially adopted by the U.S. Congress as being an official part of the U.S. Flag Code. Following World War II, President Dwight D. Eisenhower signed legislation in 1954 that added the words "under God."

Until the action by California's Ninth Circuit Court of Appeals, there had not been any type of challenge by any court regarding the words "under God." Needless to say, there was, and still is, considerable controversy regarding this ruling, which may end up being submitted to the U.S. Supreme Court for a decision.

Personally speaking, I still get a warm feeling every time I say the "Pledge of Allegiance"—and I always will.

Advertising

S ince the early 1800s, the advertising industry has used every imaginable form of patriotic images, especially images of the American flag and Uncle Sam, to advertise products on trade signs, food containers, beer and soft drink trays, coffee and tobacco containers, and other items such as mirrors, pens, paperweights, trade cards, calendars, and magazines.

With respect to Uncle Sam collectibles, hundreds if not thousands of merchants have used and promoted the image of Uncle Sam in the process of advertising their products. The quality of the Uncle Sam likeness, and the actual product and condition of the items, are important indicators of the value of these items. Because of the many collectible items that now exist, the collector who has an interest in patriotic advertising memorabilia will find that the selection is never-ending.

Advertising Trade Card
Major's Cement, 3" x 4-¹/₄", two American flags decorating display of 125-pound weights holding suspended object, full-color advertisement: "Major's Leather Cement-For-Sale by Druggists and Crockery Dealers." $10-$15

Advertising Trade Card
Uncle Sam holding shoe saying, "Hub Gore Makers of Elastic For Shoes . . . It Was Honored At The World's Fair of 1893," 3-¹/₂" x 6-¹/₄". $10-$15

Advertising Sign
"Use Jaxon Soap," Uncle Sam leaning on fence, jackknife in hand, whittling on stick. $25-$30

Advertising Sign, 1910
National Sign Company, Dayton, Ohio, canvas sign of Uncle Sam selling U.S. Paint, 16" x 24". $600-$700

American Brands, Inc., Summary of Annual Stockholders Meeting, May 6, 1976
Picture of Uncle Sam smoking a cigar and smiling, 8-^{1}/$_2$" x 6-^{1}/$_2$". $10-$15

American Eagle Fire Insurance Company, New York
Picture of bald eagle above sign reading, "American Eagle Fire Insurance Company, New York," painted tin sign with wood frame, 20-^{1}/$_2$" x 26-^{1}/$_2$". $800-$900

American Express Company Agency
Raised lettering, heavy porcelain sign, 18-^{1}/$_2$" x 16-^{1}/$_2$", U.S. flag in middle in shape of shield. Excellent condition. $1500-$1600

Automotive license plate sign, Mobil Gas, 1943, $85-$100

Babbitt's Soap Powder
Cardboard (colored) lithograph trade card with graphics of Uncle Sam and gold miners, 5-^{1}/$_2$" x 4". Excellent condition. $75-$100

Banner. New York Yankees, 1940
Banner has picture of Uncle Sam, bound in gold felt, 8" x 26". $60-$75

Barber Pole
Porcelain pole, red, white, and blue, 6" x 29". Excellent condition. $250-$275

Barber Pole
Light-up porcelain pole (red, white, and blue) with glass cylinder and top globe, 13" x 87". Excellent condition. $2500-$3500

Barbershop Sign
Advertising sign, three-piece sign consisting of heavy milk glass globe, center cast-iron bracket, bottom milk glass (red, white, and blue) striped pole, 11-^{1}/$_2$ " x 31". Excellent condition. $900-$1100

Beer Tray. West End Brewing Company, Kaufmann & Strauss Company
Beer tray, 13" diameter, American flag draped over Lady Liberty, standing next to keg of West End Brewing Company beer. $200-$250

Calendar with thermometer, Barba's Filling Station, East Warren, Rhode Island, 1943, $35-$50

Betsy Ross 5¢ Cigar
Advertisement, self-framed tin signed with picture of Betsy Ross holding the U.S. flag, 20" x 24". Very good condition. $500-$600

Brother Jonathan Chewing Tobacco, F. F. Adams Tobacco Company, Milwaukee, Wisconsin, Early 1800s
Picture of Brother Jonathan sitting in tobacco patch. $900-$1000
Brother Jonathan is thought possibly to be an early image of Uncle Sam.

Calendar with thermometer, gold-tone frame, Beiter's Market, Carroll, Iowa, 1943, $30-$45

Calendar. Union Metallic Cartridge Company, 1899
Advertising calendar with graphics of Teddy Roosevelt and the 1st Cavalry Rough Riders with American flags, ships, and soldier in background and front of calendar, 13-^{1}/$_2$" x 28". $425-$450

Case
Cast-iron advertising eagle that is sitting on top of red and blue world, 57-^{1}/$_2$" tall. $2600-$2800

Change Tray. Hebburn House Coal
Eagle in center holding banner, wood-grain background, 4". $40-$50

Clock. Acro Scientific Products Company, Illinois
Clock is cardboard, 5-^{1}/$_2$" x 7-^{1}/$_4$", with "God Bless America" on front with the map of the United States behind the Statue of Liberty, airplane propellers for clock hands. $150-$200

Columbia Match Holder
Embossed die-cut tin, wall-hung advertising piece promoting Columbia Flour, in the shape of Miss Liberty with a red, white, and blue dress, 2-^{1}/$_2$" x 5-^{1}/$_2$". Excellent condition. $900-$1100

Cigar box, Uncle Sam's Hot Shot, 1-⅞" x 7-⅜", 1918, $50-$75; Union Leader, Redi Cut Tobacco tin (middle top), 1915, $90-$115; Small Union Leader, Redi Cut Tobacco tins, 1917, $60-$70 (each); Universal Blend Coffee, 1870, $200-$250; gravy boat (right of cigar box), 1868, $1200-$1500; covered dishes (two-bottom shelf), 1898, $125-$140 (each)

Defense Bonds
"This Year give a share in America," frame poster with artwork of Santa Claus promoting bonds and stamps, 24" x 30". Excellent condition. $75-$85

Doan's Directory of the United States, Peace and Plenty, Foster-Milbur Company, Buffalo, New York, 1910
Picture of Uncle Sam sitting by shield with stars and stripes pointing to a map of the United States. $75-$85

"Drink Solo, High in Quality, 6 Fruity Flavors"
Picture of fighter pilot with plane in background. $50-$60

"Duty Calls," 1917
World War I paper advertisement with U.S. flag in background reflecting doughboy leaving home for war. Good condition. $150-$200

Eisenhower Cigarettes, "I Like Ike," 1950s
Picture of President Dwight D. Eisenhower on pack of cigarettes with red and white packaging. $75-$85

Fan. Ontario Drill Company, Baltimore, Maryland, 1908
Full eagle front, 8" x 9". $75-$85

Fan. Red Star Line Folding Fan, Antwerp, New York, 1900
Fan opens up to American flag, 8-½" x 16" x 1". $30-$40

Fanny Farmer Candy Cylinder, 1944
Cylinder is Uncle Sam with wooden arms, hat (labeled "Fanny Farmer") pulls off, 10-⅝" x 3". $85-$100

"Here's the Inside Story of the 1938 Pontiac, American's Finest Low-Priced Car," 1937
Picture of smiling Uncle Sam with Indian; inside folds show various views of the car, 20-¼" x 12-⅞". $60-$70

Picture, Daniel Scotten & Company, Harmony Chewing Tobacco, Detroit, Michigan, 1879, 10-⁵/₈" x 13-³/₈", $1200-$1500; collapsible display box, The *Big* Tin, Union Leader, the *Best* Tobacco Value, New Style-New Cut, 1916, 18-¹/₂" x 17-¹/₂", rare, $3000-$3500

"I'd Give a Month's Pay for a Dr. Pepper, Good for Life," 1943 (World War II)
Picture of soldier riding in tank with dollars in his hand, cardboard poster in wood frame, 28-¹/₂" x 18-¹/₂". $350-$375

Independent Gasoline
Gas globe depicting image of "Spirit of 76" painting (drummer, fife, and boy carrying American flag), red metal molding with two glass lenses, 15" diameter. Rare. $5000-$5500

Independent Local and Long Distance Telephone
Double-sided porcelain sign with red, white, and blue background with stars and stripes. $550-$600

Jacob Metzger, American Brewing Company, Indianapolis, Indiana
Beer tray, 12" diameter, trademark on star in center of flag. $125-$150

Lapel Stud. Harrison/Morton, 1888
Red, white, and blue enamel flag, white background. $25-$35

Magazine Tear Sheet, 1915
Uncle Sam holding a health bill under his arm, looking at Cream of Wheat advertising billboard, 5-¹/₂" x 8-¹/₂". $20-$25

"Man As He Says," National Biscuit Company, August 10, 1918
Picture of Uncle Sam holding boxes of biscuits and crackers, 10" x 6". $50-$60

Mason & Mason Exclusive Woolens-Victory (Postcard), 1919
Advertising calendar, James W. Taylor, Arcadia, Pennsylvania, with background of soldiers, rifles, Statue of Liberty, flying eagle. Excellent condition. $50-$60

Matchbox, 1861-1865
Embossed picture of Stars and Stripes on one side, Miss Columbia on reverse side, 1-¹/₂" x 2-³/₄". $55-$65

Advertising calendar, Mason & Johnson—Exclusive Woolens, James W. Allen, Arcadia, Pennsylvania, 1919, excellent condition, $50-$60

Match Cover. Karmelkorn, Chicago Heights, Illinois
Uncle Sam holding a finger over his lips, saying "Careless lips . . . can sink ships." $4-$5

Match Holder. Unitus Uncle Sam Cigars, 1918
Wall-hanging match holder, molded plaster, hand-painted face of Uncle Sam, 6-$^1/_2$" diameter. $250-$400

Merrick's Thread
Two infant children, one beating Civil War drum, the other waving flag, titled "Young America." $5-$7

Ohio Rake Company, Dayton
Vintage paper lithograph with graphics depicting Statue of Liberty and patriotic farming scenes, 34-$^1/_2$" x 28-$^1/_2$". $2000-$2300

Pilgrim Shoe and Rubber Company, Boston, Massachusetts(Postcard), 1917
Photograph of President Wilson with U.S. flag in background. $40-$45

Pin. Hupmobile, the Car of the American Family on United America Tour
Celluloid, die-cut, red, white, and blue shield design, dark gold eagle. $35-$45

Pinback Buttons
★ **Federal Casualty Insurance, Detroit, Michigan**
   Multicolored, $^3/_4$", Uncle Sam, money pouring from horn of plenty. $20-$25
★ **Hop Ale, 1907**
   Displays American flag and shield. $10-$15
★ **National Relief Assurance Company, Philadelphia, Pennsylvania**
   Multicolored eagle and Liberty Bell, dark blue background. $20-$25
★ **Peitler Patriot Publishing Company, Denver, Colorado**
   Spanish American War, multicolored image of Uncle Sam lowering Spanish flag and raising U.S. flag, witnessed by soldier and sailor; caption: "We Have Remembered the Maine." $100-$110

Display signs: "National Advertised Sold Here," 1912, 36" x 16", $700-$900; OshKosh B'Gosh, 45" x 27", 1942, $750-$1000; Yankee Doodle, 1940, $70-$90; Mass & Stiffen fur advertisement, 1920, $175-$200

New York Yankees pennant, 1940, $100-$150; wood soap box, 1870, $300-$350; display case, $1.00 watches, 1915, $200-$300; advertising tin, coffee, 1880, $900-$1200; advertising sign, Uncle Sam, 1921, $1800-$2499

Poster. Register the Baby's Birth, "Where is the record of my Illinois children?" 1941
Poster published by the U.S. Census Bureau, Uncle Sam reviewing Census Book, 8-3/4" x 6". $30-$35

"Preparedness," Cream of Wheat, 1917
Full-color print with Uncle Sam eating a big bowl of Cream of Wheat, sitting in chair with shield of stars and stripes in background and bald eagle perched on shield, 11-1/2" x 9-1/2". $50-$60

Puzzle. Uncle Sam's Tar Soap, 1900
Uncle Sam's National Puzzle, 4" x 4" box, 10 cards, advertising slogans. $25-$30

Roosevelt Scoured Africa, the Gold Dust Twins Scour America—"Let the Gold Dust Twins do your work," 1900
Stone lithograph on paper on hardboard; picture depicts Uncle Sam reaching out to Roosevelt with Gold Dust Twins carrying bags, 13" x 26". $6000-$6500

Shredded Wheat, An International Agreement, The Natural Food Company, Niagara Falls, New York, Toronto, Canada, London, England, April 16, 1905
Picture of Uncle Sam shaking hands with English gentlemen, 14" x 11". $65-$85

Sign. "Protect Your Hands with Yankee Doodle Gloves and Mittens," Galena Glove & Mitten Company, The Sign of Quality, Dubuque, Iowa, 1940
Sign with picture of Uncle Sam whistling with hands in pocket, printed on heavy composition cardboard, 14-^{1}/$_2$" x 20". $70-$90

Sign. Providence Washington Insurance Company
Picture depicting George Washington, tin advertising sign with wood frame, 20-^{1}/$_2$" x 26-^{1}/$_2$". $325-$350

Souvenir of Teddy's Visit, 1910
America's most distinguished citizen (front), "America's Greatest Headache Remedy" Gladstone sold by leading druggists (postcard), published by Gladstone Manufacturing Company, Sioux City, Iowa. Excellent condition. $100-$150

Statement January 1, 1921, Capital, Reserve, Surplus, Assets—Thoroughly American Institution, 1921
Metal sign depicting serious Uncle Sam with background of red and stripes, 12-^{1}/$_8$" x 13-^{1}/$_8$". $2400-$2700

Stick Pin. Artistic Pianos, early 1900-1920
Die-cut celluloid red, white, and blue American flag on front, black and white advertising on back. $25-$30

The Talk of the Hour, America Flour, It-Is-The-Electric-Light-Of-Milling, Yours Truly, Jas Wilson Company, Rochester, New York, 1903
Picture of Uncle Sam holding shield of red, white, and blue stars and stripes, 14-^{7}/$_8$" x 10-^{1}/$_2$". $100-$125

Tins
★ **E. B. Miller & Company**
  Uncle Sam image on coffee tin, 6-^{1}/$_2$" high, 4" deep, 1 pound. $45-$50
★ **Uncle Sam's High Grade Roasted Coffee, Thomas Wood and Company Importers and Roasters, Boston, 1880**
  General store bulk display advertising tin with roll-back door. $900-$1200
★ **Uncle Sam Tobacco Tins, Union Leader Redi-Cut Tobacco (five tins), 1915-1917**
  Back reads "Genuine Union Leader Redi-Cut, Specialty prepared for pipe and cigarette." $50-$60 (each)
★ **Wiles Biscuit Company, Bakers of Sunshine Biscuits, New York**
  Signing of Constitution, Gold Rush, Statue of Liberty. $25-$30

Tip Tray. Grand Old Party, 1856-1908
Round tip tray with artwork of Taft & Sherman in center of tray under graphics of White House, 4-$^1/_8$". $85-$95

Trade Cards
★ **Brother Jonathan, Centennial Exposition, 1876**
Standing among sale items at Exposition. Artist: Thomas Nast. $65-$80
Brother Jonathan is thought to possibly be an early image of Uncle Sam.
★ **"Buy The United States Playing Cards," Manufactured by the Russell & Morgan Printing Company, Cincinnati, Ohio, 1875-1885**
U.S. flag with large star surrounded by small stars. $20-$30
★ **"The Compliments Of The Season Cousin," D. P. Ives & Company, Importers of Fine Goods and Toilet Articles, 26 Franklin Street, Boston, Massachusetts, 1878**
Picture of Uncle Sam with eagle talking to another person. $30-$40
★ **Cosack & Company, Publishers of Advertising Specialties, 1890**
U.S. flag. $20-$30
★ **DeGrauw Aymar & Company, Flags, American Ensigns, Jacks, Signal, Burgee, Etc., Every Description of Best Quality Flag Work, 1880**
Picture of American flag. $25-$30
★ **Dr. Ward's Celebrated Jersey Corn Salve, "A Positive and Painless Cure For Hand & Soft Corns, Bunions, Warts, Moles, Callouses, Etc." Price 15¢, 1895**
Picture of American flag with "Corn Salve" on flag. $35-$45
★ **"Fairbank's Fairy Soap, The Two Best Things That Float, Pure White, Floating," 1895**
Picture of American flag. $25-$30
★ **Frank Millers Blacking, 1882**
Uncle Sam shaving with straight razor, using polished boot as mirror, eagle looking at reflection in another boot. $25-$30
★ **Highest Gold Medal Awarded, Hub Gore Makers, Elastic for Shoes, Columbian Exposition, 1893**
"Uncle Sam, the Wonderful Edison Talking Automation at World Fair, delivering 40,000 speeches during the Exhibition, about Highest Award, Gold Medal, Hub Gore," 3-$^5/_8$" x 6". $35-$45
★ **Ideal Felt Tooth Polisher, 1880**
U.S. flag. $30-$40
★ **King's Flour, "Use Hygienic Kalsomine," 1903**
Picture of Uncle Sam passing out packages of King's Flour. $25-$30

★ Ladies Pocket Calendar, "Clark's Thread," 1879
Uncle Sam handing out Clark's thread to women of international origin, 2-⁵/₈" x 4-³/₈". $40-$50

★ Mahler & Thomson, Jobbers in Carriages, Harness, Sewing Machines, and Agricultural Implements, St. Paul, Minnesota, 1890
Full-color stone lithograph with Uncle Sam sitting down by large picture of United States gold coin certificate, 2-³/₄" x 3-¹/₂". $25-$30

★ National Refining Company, Cleveland, Ohio, National Light Oil, The National Refining Company, 1882
Uncle Sam and Miss Liberty endorsing "White Rose Stove Gasoline," 3-¹/₄" x 6". $40-$50

★ They Return >From Dives, Pomery & Steward, J & P Coats Best Six Cord, 1876
Uncle Sam with a Scotsman carrying a large coin, 2-¹/₂ x 3-⁷/₈". $35-$45

★ Uncle Sam's Harness Oil, C. Drake, Rushford, Minnesota, Dealer in Harness, Saddles, Collars, Bridles, Whips, etc., 1878
Uncle Sam holding can of oil with stable workers and horse in background, 3" x 5". $35-$45

★ Uncle Sam Supplying the World with Berry Brothers, Architectural Finishes, 1880
Picture of Uncle Sam handing out cans of Berry Varnishes, 3-¹/₂" x 5-⁵/₈". $40-$45

★ Universal Ammoniated Dissolved Bones, Williams Clark & Company's High Grade Bone Fertilizer, 1880
Picture of American flag with gold crown in star area of flag. $20-$25

★ Williams Genuine Yankee Soap, J. B. Williams & Company, 1880-1890
Picture of American flag. $20-$25

Uncle Sam Advertising Bank
Issued by Poll Parrot Shoes, red, white, and blue, lithograph cardboard, silvered tin cap and bottom, 2-¹/₄" x 3". $50-$75

Uncle Sam Bank, Toy and Novelty Company
Gold, 9-³/₈" x 4-⁵/₈" x 2-³/₈". $125-$150

Uncle Sam Brand, Yakima Valley Apples, Packed by Wapato Fruit & Cold Storage Company, Wapato, Washington, 1918
Label with border of apples and Uncle Sam hats, picture on label of Uncle Sam holding his hat, 9" x 11". $40-$50

Uncle Sam Cigar Box, 1918

Cigar box with American flag and shield with stars and stripes, red bottom, 1-⁷/₈" x 11" x 7-³/₈". $100-$125

OshKosh store display, 1942, $400-$600; Uncle Sam die-cut cardboard store display, Dutch Boy Paint, 48-³/₈" x 25-³/₈", 1918, $1200-$1500

Uncle Sam "Jr. Savings Bank and Clock"

Red leather clock hands, bank box is tin, 8" x 8-¹/₂". $150-$175

Uncle Sam Plaque, "Save for Victory," Bank

Glass bubble to hold coins in front of picture, Uncle Sam in the middle with flags on both sides of picture, cardboard, wood, and glass, 7-¹/₈" x 11". $150-$185

Uncle Sam Stock Medicine Company, Quincy, Illinois, 1919

Heavy paper with patriotic images of Statue of Liberty and naval ships returning home, 15" x 20". Near mint condition. $200-$250

Union Leader, Tobacco

Tin lithograph Union Leader Tobacco sign with bald eagle in center, 10-¹/₂" x 15". $225-$250

U.S. Playing Card Company, Cincinnati, Ohio

Playing cards, "606"—Picture of Statue of Liberty and flags of nations, gold edges. $20-$25

Watch Fob. American Badge Company, 1900

Raised eagle on front, red, white, and blue enameled name, American Badge Company, shield shape, attached silvered brass horseshoe. $45-$55

Watch Fob. Dedication Uncle Sam Oakwood Cemetery, 1930-1935

Brass, 1-¹/₄" x 1-¹/₂", raised portrait of Uncle Sam above VFW symbol. $20-$25

Waterman's Ideal Fountain Pen, "The National Pen—In The Vest Pocket of the World," 1939

Picture of Uncle Sam using pen and writing, 1939 magazine advertisement, 10" x 7". $15-$20

"WE CAN! WE WILL! WE MUST!"
Let's work harder at our jobs and do them better.
BROWN & BIGELOW
ST. PAUL, MINN.

Calendar, Brown & Bigelow, St. Paul, Minnesota, 1943, $65-$85

"We, too, have a job to do—Join a Boy Scout Troop, Boy Scouts of America, An Opportunity For All Boys To Serve America," 1943
Paper lithograph poster depicting Boy Scouts, Cub Scouts, Navy and Army men, lady dressed like Statue of Liberty carrying torch and plaque reading "Bill of Rights, American Flags and Boy Scout Flags," 19-3/4" x 29-1/2". $300-$325

Zippo Lighter, Uncle Sam Cereal, A Natural Laxative, "Thanks John McGowan," 1952
Picture of Uncle Sam cereal box on the side of Zippo lighter, 2-1/4" x 1-1/2". $35-$45

Modern Patriotic Artwork

*A*rt has always provided a rich and deep patriotic depiction of the many expressions and emotions of our country, documenting major events beginning with the birth of America in 1776 and every defining significant event for each generation. And once again, the world of art has risen to the occasion to reflect the patriotism in an art form reminiscent of World War II–era posters and sculptures. This chapter will be devoted to two separate and unique modern works of art depicting patriotism at its very best: "Art Fights Back," a collection by artist John Sayles, Sayles Graphic Design, Des Moines, Iowa, and the "American Patriot," Tiffany glass and sculpture collection by Meyda Tiffany, Yorkville, New York.

"Art Fights Back"

"Art Fights Back" is a collection of posters and banners that were inspired by the events of September 11, 2001, to honor the military, public servants, the spirit of America, and the patriotism of every American. Designed by artist John Sayles, these posters and banners are a historical link to another similar project: the World War II–era posters of the Works Progress Administration (WPA). This project began with one poster, with the thought that it could help to promote the issuance of War Bonds. But as the creativity and ink transferred to paper, it quickly became apparent that the project could serve a much larger purpose.

Following the terrorist attacks in New York and Washington, more than 30 Des Moines, Iowa–area businesses came together to participate in an effort that resulted in 30 original works of art being developed between September 11 and late November. Proceeds from the sales of the initial exhibition on December 7, 2001 benefited the Armed Forces Services fund, which supports America's military men and women and their families. According to Sheree Clark, spokesperson and cofounder of Sayles Graphic Design, the idea of holding the exhibition and sharing the posters and banners with the public was important for two reasons: "First, it gave our community a chance to really reflect on what happened in America these past few months, and second, it is a fantastic opportunity to raise funds and support for those who are defending and protecting our country." I think that summarizes the feeling quite well. Enjoy the art.

Banners

"Bin Laden Declared War, We Will End It, Defeat Terrorism"
Red hand with fingers formed in "V" symbol and bombs dropping in background, 50" x 9'. $2000

"At War, At Home," 2001, 50" x 9', $2000

"Dear God, Keep U.S. Safe, Issue War Bonds"
Soldier with helmet (flag in center) with gas mask, 50" x 9'. $2000

"Fill the Void with Justice"
Lady Liberty with flaming torch and light beams shining down, 50" x 9'. $2000

"The Giant Is Awake and Fighting Mad, He Will Not Rest Unanswered"
Uncle Sam rolling up his sleeves with fist clenched, U.S. flag is lower right-hand corner, 50" x 9'. $2000

"God Help Us in the Face of Evil"
Sinister-looking Bin Laden surrounded by flames, 50" x 9'. $2000

"Let 'em Have It, Issue War Bonds"
Eagle with banner in mouth ("Let 'em Have It") with talons around bomb falling toward red and white target, other bombs falling in background, 50" x 9'. $2000

"God Bless America," 2001,
50" x 9', $2000

"Let Freedom Ring, Stop Terrorism"
Abstract depiction of Uncle Sam ringing bell of freedom, 50" x 9'. $2000

"Let's Go USA, Keep 'em Flying, Issue War Bonds"
Hand of Uncle Sam pointing skyward to fighter planes, 50" x 9'. $2000

"Not an Age of Terror, an Age of Liberty"
Illustration depicting bomb on top half and two men raising U.S. flag on bottom half, 50" x 9'. $2000

"Only Cowards Kill and Hide"
Twin Towers surrounded by flames with red hand wrapped around a commercial jet aircraft, 50" x 9'. $2000

"Printed on Our Heart Forever, Extra, Extra"
Newspaper carrier holding paper with headline "Terror," 50" x 9'. $2000

Public Servants, **"P.S. We [picture of heart] You"**
Smiling firefighter, 50" x 9'. $2000

Public Servants, **"P.S. We [picture of heart] You"**
Smiling woman police officer, 50" x 9'. $2000

Public Servants, **"P.S. We [picture of heart] You"**
Smiling postal worker delivering letter, 50" x 9'. $2000

"Terrorism, It Will Not Stand, Twin Towers Fall, NY, NY"
Uncle Sam standing over fallen Twin Towers, 50" x 9'. $2000

"Liberty and Justice for All,"
2001, 50" x 9', $2000

"At the Ready, At War, At Home,"
2001, 17-½" x 37-½", $40

"Under Attack, Sept 11, 2001, Terrorist Target America"
Twin Towers in scope sights with blue jet heading for towers, 50" x 9'. $2000

"U.S.A., Protect What We Have"
Eagle with U.S. flag in background, 50" x 9'. $2000

"The War on Fear Begins Here, Defeat Terrorism"
Bomber dropping bombs within picture of red heart-shaped apple, 50" x 9'. $2000

Posters

"Indivisible with Liberty and Justice for All"
Buildings in city and U.S. flag flying above the Lincoln Memorial, 17-¹/₂" x 37-¹/₂". $40

"God Bless America," 2001,
17-½" x 37-½", $40

"I Pledge Allegiance to the Flag,"
2001, 17-½" x 37-½", $150

"Remember That Day,
September 11, 2001," 2001,
17-½" x 37-½", $150

"Stand Beside Her and Guide Her,
United We Stand," 2001,
17-½" x 37-½", $40

"The Land of the Free and the Home of the Brave, In Memory of Those Who Died September 11, 2001"
Large "11" in the center of an American eagle, 17-¹/₂" x 9'. $40

"Mr. President, the Heartland Is Behind You"
Uncle Sam and the president together with farmlands and city in the background, 17-¹/₂" x 37-¹/₂". $40

"United We Stand, Together They Fall, Stop Terrorism, September 11, 2001"
World Trade Center Twin Towers in red, white, and blue with a blue star on each tower, 17-¹/₂" x 37-¹/₂". $40

"Weep, Remember, But Fear Not"
Uncle Sam with a black eye, looking sad but determined, 17-¹/₂" x 37-¹/₂". $150

"American Patriot" Glass and Sculpture Collection

As with the artwork of "Art Fights Back," Meyda Tiffany, a leading designer and manufacturer of Tiffany lamps and decorative lighting, introduced the "American

Patriot" collection to benefit numerous American relief organizations helping and assisting victims and their families affected by the tragic events of September 11, 2001. The "American Patriot" collection includes American flag lighted sculptures, fan lites, and stained-glass windows depicting "Old Glory" and the bald eagle. The American flag and eagle lamps were handcrafted of fine art glass using Tiffany's famous copperfoil construction process. Enjoy the "American Patriot" collection.

"Star Spangled America the Beautiful,"
2002, stained-glass window,
22" high x 17" wide, $375

Angel of Glory Fan Lamp
Fused image of an angel with the American flag on stained glass, 6" high. $50

Old Glory Fan Lamp
Fused color image of the American flag on glass that is wrapped in solid brass, 5" high. $50

"Old Glory" Table Lamp
Fused color image of the American flag on an art glass shade (all four sides) wrapped in solid brass, 15" high. $100

American Flag and Eagle Accent Lamp,
2002, Tiffany sculpture with fine art glass,
11-½" high, 10" long, $150

Bottles and Glass

With the beginning of World War II, the bottling industry, specifically the milk-bottling manufacturers, began a campaign of patriotism in America that had never been experienced before at any time of history. World War II resulted in some of the most unique and collectible bottles, with war slogans depicting tanks, soldiers, fighter planes, "V" signs, and sayings and slogans about Pearl Harbor. While many of the bottles, especially milk bottles, were very colorful with many detailed graphics, the war slogans were mainly quite basic, with sayings like "Buy Bonds and Stamps" and "Buy War Savings Bonds—Keep It Up" on the wings of bombers and fighter planes.

Along with milk bottles, the applied color label (ACL) soda pop bottle, which was conceived in the 1930s when Prohibition forced brewing companies to experiment with soda pop, also featured war slogans. Bottlers throughout the United States created bottle labels that will forever preserve unique patriotic moments and figures in American history, including the American flag, the Statue of Liberty, and stars and stripes. Those bottles with images of Uncle Sam and the American flag are the most popular.

Other groups of bottles, such as historical flasks, figurals, and Jim Beam bottles, have depicted patriotic figures, embossed images, and paintings of important patriotic milestones in the history of America.

Milk Bottles

Quarts 1942–1945

Anderson Erickson Dairy, Des Moines, Iowa
Picture of Abraham Lincoln, "That Freedom shall not perish from the earth!"
"Buy War Bonds." $100-$125

Clarksburg Dairy, Clarksburg, West Virginia
"Conserve 'V' for Victory, Buy War Bonds and Stamps." $85-$100

Cloverleaf Dairy, Maryland
Red stars around bottle, bomber with "Buy War Savings Bonds" on wings,
"Keep It Up." $75-$100

Compston Bros. Dairy, Corning, California
Black lettering, "Milk for Victory" with "V" symbol. $75-$100

Crane Dairy, Utica, New York
Red lettering, "Buy War Bonds and Stamps For Victory." $45-$55

"Keep 'em Flying, Buy a Bond
Today, Army Flyers Drink Milk,"
1943. $65-$75

Dykes Dairy, Warren, Pennsylvania
"The United States is a Good Investment
[picture of Statue of Liberty], Buy War Bonds
and Stamps." $75-$85

Elmwood Dairy, Oxbridge, Massachusetts
"We Need Your Help [Uncle Sam pointing],
It's Your Right, It's Your Responsibility,
Buy More Bonds." $60-$70

Ferry Hills Farms, Prairie View, Illinois
"It's Patriotic to Save [picture of fighter plane],
Buy War Bonds and Stamps." $75-$85

Geneva Dairy, Geneva, New York
"'V' For Victory," with sailor standing by battleship.
$75-$100

Golden Crest, Bordens
"Buy War Bonds." $75-$100

Hansen Dairy, Deer Lodge, Montana
Black lettering, "Bonds Buy Bombs." $75-$100

Haskels Dairy, Augusta, California
"Back Their Attack, Buy More War Bonds, Drink Milk For Health." $50-$60

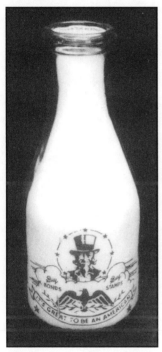

Haskels Dairy, Augusta, California
"Milk Helps To Keep 'em Flying, Do Your Part, Buy War Bonds and Stamps," with picture of a pilot. $75-$85

Heisler's Cloverleaf Dairy, Tamaqua, Pennsylvania
"Armaments and Good Health, For Victory, Drink More Milk." $100-$125

HyGrade Dairy, Buffalo, New York
"Give A Pint of Blood And Help Save A Life." Rare. $175-$200

Illinois Valley, Strator, Ottawa, Illinois
Orange lettering, "Revenge Pearl Harbor." $75-$100

Kentucky Acres Dairy, Crestwood, Kentucky
"Buy War Bonds, Everybody, Every Payday," on arrow pointing to target. $50-$60

Maple Grove Dairy, Maple Grove, Illinois, 1943, $75-$85

Lavine's Dairy, Potsdam, New York
"Victory," with picture of soldier in middle of "V." $75-$100

Melrose Dairy, Dyersburg, Tennessee
Red lettering, fighter plane, "Keep 'Em Flying, Buy War Bonds Today." $100-$125

Perry Creamery, Tuscaloosa, Alabama
"National Defense Starts, Buy Defense Bonds, With Health Defense." $60-$75

Shamrock Dairy, Tucson, Arizona
"America Has A Job To Do!" "V" symbol with picture of pilot. $75-$100

Shums Dairy, Jeanette, Pennsylvania
Picture of eagle, "National Defense Starts With Good Health, Build America's Future, Drink More Milk." $35-$45

Sunshine Dairy, St. Johns, Newfoundland, Canada
Black and orange lettering, Victory Sign with Churchill, tanks, and ships. $200-$250

Thatchers Manufacturing Glass Company, Series of Eight Slogans $100-$150 (each)
★ "Victory Comes a Little Closer Every Time You Buy a War Bond,"
  with fighter plane.
★ "We Need Your Help, It's Your Fight, It's Your Responsibility, Buy War Bonds,"
  with Uncle Sam pointing.
★ **Anderson Erickson Dairy, Des Moines, Iowa**
  "That Freedom Shall Not Perish From the Earth!, Buy War Bonds,"
  (Abraham Lincoln).
★ "Think, Act, Work [picture of eagle], Victory."
★ "You Can Keep 'Em Flying By Buying [picture of fighter plane]
  U.S. War Bonds-Stamps."
★ "Action Speaks Louder Than Words, What Are You Doing to Help Uncle Sam?"
★ **Royale Dairy, Elmira, New York**
  "Keep Them Rolling [picture of tank], Buy Bonds and Stamps."
★ "You Owe It To Your Country, Buy War Bonds, You Owe It To Your Health,
  Drink Milk."

Common Quarts

"A Healthy Nation Is A Strong Nation," Uncle Sam holding a glass of milk. $35-$45

"AMERICA Is A Great Place To Be, Let's Keep It That Way." $35-$40

"Buy Defense Bonds and Stamps For Victory," with "V" symbol. $45-$55

"50th Anniversary of Pearl Harbor," Made for Collectors Market, 1992. $15-$20

"Food Fights Too [picture of Uncle Sam], Conserve What You Buy, Plan All
Meals For Victory." $45-$50

"For Our Defense, Battleship, 1200 Men." $50-$55

"God Bless America," "Pearl Harbor Remembered," "Made For Collectors
Market," 1992. $15-$20

"Help Save The Life Of A Soldier or Sailor [picture of red cross], Donate To The
Blood Plasma Program Of The Red Cross." Rare. $200-$250

"It's Great To Be An American," with picture of Uncle Sam and eagle. $35-$45

"Invest In Victory [picture of bombers], War Savings Bonds-Stamps." $75-$100

"Remember Pearl Harbor, Safe Guard Your Country By Doing Your Bit Now, Be Prepared," with "V" symbol. $125-$150

Uncle Sam pointing to three signs: "Your Country First," "Your Family Second," "Yourself Last." $45-$55

"U.S. Savings Bonds and Freedom Shares." $20-$25

"We Cherish Liberty, Health, Let's Protect Them," 1943. $35-$45

Cream Tops

Common Bottles
★ "Food For Victory, Careful Wartime Meal Planning Will Help Us Win." $75-$100
★ "Making It Together [picture of Uncle Sam and milkman], An American Tradition." $35-$45
★ "Uncle Sam Prescribes Milk For The Army." Rare. $150-$200
★ "'V' For Victory, Guernsey Milk For Health." $75-$85

Gateway Dairy
"My WAR STAMPS Are Adding Up." $85-$95

Shamrock Dairy, Tucson, Arizona
"America Has A Job To Do," "V" symbol with fighter pilot. $75-$100

Walnut Grove Dairy, Alton, Illinois
"Buy War Bonds and Stamps For Victory." $75-$95

Half-Pints

Alden's Dairy
"Speed Victory." $25-$30

Common Bottles
★ "Do Your Part Too! Buy War Bonds & Stamps." $35-$40
★ "War Bonds For Victory." $20-$25
★ "You Can Keep Them Flying By Buying U.S. War Bonds and Stamps." $30-$35

Dairylea Dairy
"Buy Bonds For Victory." $35-$45

Live Oak Riviera Farms, Santa Barbara, California
USA food emblem, red and blue, flying eagle surrounded by stars. $35-$40

Beer Bottles

"Buy U.S. War Bonds," Metz Brewing Company
9-1/2". $25-$35

Pioneer "Victory" Beer
9-1/2". $25-$35

Uncle Sam Beer, Glencoe Brewing Company, Glencoe, Minnesota, 1918
Amber, 9-1/4", two paper labels with picture depicting Uncle Sam holding a bottle
of beer next to the brewery, 14 ounces. $125-$150

Figurals

Independence Hall Bank, "Bank Of Independence Hall 1776–1876," Patent
Pending
Pressed clear glass, 7-1/4", tin base sliding closure. $375-$475
American 1876 (Rare souvenir candy container from the Philadelphia Centennial
Exposition of 1876.)

Liberty Bell Candy Container, "Proclaim Liberty Throughout The Land-1776/
Centennial Exposition/1876"
Clear, 3-1/2", smooth base, sheared and ground lip. $175-$275
American 1875–1876

Liberty Dollar Coin Flask
On one side "United States Of America/In God We Trust" (American eagle)/one
dollar, on other side "E. Pluribus Unum"/(bust of Columbia), clear, 4-1/2", smooth
base, ground lip. $250-$350
American 1885–1895

Military Hat Candy Container
Clear, cap reading "U.S. Military Hat, Pla-Toy Company," Greensburg,
Pennsylvania. $80-$140
American 1930–1940

Statue of Liberty Jars (two jars)

Both clear glass, 12-$^1/_2$", smooth base, ground rims. $275-$375
American 1886–1890 (Brought from France in 1885 and unveiled on October 28, 1886. President Cleveland received this gift from France for the American people.)

Statue of Liberty

Milk glass base with cast metal Statue of Liberty, 15-$^1/_2$" (including statue), smooth base, sheared and ground lip. $400-$500
American 1890–1900

Uncle Sam

Clear, 9-$^1/_2$", smooth base, tooled top, "tall hat" screw-on cap. $80-$120
American 1890–1910

Uncle Sam Candy Container

Clear glass with 50% of original red, white, and blue paint, Uncle Sam standing next to container. $300-$400
American 1915–1925

Flask, eagle with Stars and Stripes shield, dark green pint, 1825–1835, $300-$500

Flasks

Ceramic G.A.R. Presidents Flask

White with multicolored transfers of GAR Medal on one side depicting Lincoln (April 14, 1865), and on the reverse, Garfield (July 2, 1884) and McKinley (September 6, 1901), 5-$^3/_4$". $350-$450
A rare flask showing the three presidents, who were assassinated while in office.

Eagle with Banner

Medium yellow–olive green quart, smooth base, applied top. $500-$800
American 1855–1860

Eagle – Eagle

Greenish aqua pint, pontil scarred base, sheared lip. $150-$200
American 1835–1845

Flask, eagle with Stars and Stripes shield, light aqua pint, 1835–1845. $150-$200

Eagle, Furled Flag, "For Our Country"
Medium yellow-green pint, pontil scarred base, tooled lip. Rare. $1500-$2500
American 1825–1835

Eagle, "Liberty" Tree
Light green half-pint, pontil scarred base, tooled top. $700-$900
American 1820–1835

"Liberty"/Eagle, Willington Glass Company, West Willington, Connecticut
Deep olive-green pint, smooth base, applied sloping collar top. $200-$300
American 1865–1875

Jim Beam Bottles

American Bald Eagle, 1966
White head, golden beak, and rich brown plumage, yellow claws gripping a branch of a tree. $25-$35

AMVETS, 1970
Commemorates the 25th anniversary of the veterans of American wars: World War II, the Korean War, and the Vietnam War. Gold metal eagle designed for stopper above the red, white, blue, and yellow bottle. Embossed war scene is on the reverse. 11-³/₄". $20-$30

Bald Eagle, 1985
Bald eagle with spread wings. $25-$30

Boots and Helmet, 1984
Army helmet sitting on top of combat boots. $25-$35
Very collectible among military personnel and collectors.

Crispus Attucks, 1976
Picture of Crispus Attucks, American Revolutionary War hero, with American flag in background. $5-$10

Franklin Mint, 1970
Liberty Bell on one side and blue and white shield with "Liberty" on other side.
$5-$10

Pearl Harbor, 1972
"Dec 7, 1941, Pearl Harbor, Pearl Harbor Survivors Association," with bald eagle
sitting on top of bottle. $25-$35

Statue of Liberty, 1975
"Give me your tired . . ." on back. $20-$25

Victory beverage soda bottle,
1943, 9-½". $25-$35

Statue of Liberty, 1985
"Give me your tired . . ." on back. $20-$30

**U.S. Open, Pebble Beach, California,
June 12-18, 1972**
Red, white, and blue Uncle Sam hat doubling as a
golf bag. $25-$30

Washington State Bicentennial, 1976
Revolutionary War drummer on red and white
base with a gold Liberty Bell reading "1776–1976"
and round blue sign with stars reading
"200 Years." $15-$20

Shot Glasses and Stir Sticks

Blown-glass Uncle Sam top hat shot glasses with
blown glass stir sticks (set of six); hat 2" x 2-¼",
stir sticks 5-¼" (each). $125-$150 (set)

Soda Bottles

Dunn's Beverages, Sedalia, Missouri, 1954
Clear glass, Statue of Liberty in front of clouds, 10
ounces. $15-$20

**Liberty Bottling Company, Memphis,
Tennessee, 1950**
Green glass, Statue of Liberty, 12 ounces. $65-$85

My Pic, Alexandria, Louisiana, 1949
Clear glass, Statue of Liberty with stars erupting from torch, 10 ounces. $30-$35

Uncle Sam's Beverage, Houston, Texas, 1947
Clear glass, picture of Uncle Sam on yellow label, 7 ounces. $90-$100

Victory Root Beer, 1947
Dark glass, picture of stars and stripes, 10 ounces. $50-$65

Royal Doulton Dewar's White Label Whisky bottle, Royal Doulton, England, 1907, high-glazed porcelain with a dark brown base and dark brown top fading to a light brownish gold center, 7-¼" x 6-½" x 2-¾", $300-$400

Miscellaneous

Covered Dish, 1898
Opalescent milk glass with Uncle Sam seated between the smokestacks of the ship *USS Olympia*. The bottom of the boat has an eagle on the bow with portholes and guns on the sides.
6-$^1/_2$" x 3" x 4-$^5/_8$". $125-$150

Gravy Boat, Union Porcelain Works, Greenpoint, Brooklyn, New York, 1868
Fine porcelain gravy boat with Uncle Sam and John Bull reclining on top of boat,
7-$^1/_2$" x 3-$^1/_2$" x 5-$^1/_8$". $1200-$1500

Occupational Shaving Mug Made for "Adolph Market," 1880–1920
Picture on mug depicting a flexed arm holding a hammer in front of the American flag, maroon wrap with a gold gilt edge. $300-$400

Flags

Resolved, that a flag for the 13 United States be 13 stripes alternated red and white, with a union of 13 white stars in a blue field to represent a new constellation.

—Motion adopted by the Continental Congress in 1777 of the Stars and Stripes as the United States flag

Since the very beginnings of a young United States of America, the American flag has represented the basic principles and foundations on which our country was founded. Our flag has always served as a symbol of freedom and democracy, giving U.S. citizens a special feeling of being home and secure. With the possible exception of the bombing of Pearl Harbor on December 7, 1941, and our entry into World War II, our country has seen the most fervent passion for the flag with the recent terrorist attack on the New York World Trade Towers on September 11, 2001.

And how many other countries can boast that their national anthem is the subject of their flag, as is the case with "The Star-Spangled Banner." On September 14, 1814, when Francis Scott Key saw the American flag still flying proudly after a 25-hour British Naval bombardment of Baltimore's Fort McHenry, he was inspired to write the poem that later became our national anthem. In fact, that very flag underwent a major restoration beginning in 1999 and completed during the summer of 2002. Here are a few unknown facts about this patriotic symbol of America:

★ The red and white stripes and the blue union of the Star-Spangled Banner are made of English woolen bunting, dyed blue with indigo and red with cochineal and madder. The stars are cotton and are sewn into the union by reverse appliqué method.

★ Each star is about 2 feet across and each stripe is about 23 inches wide.

★ In 1914 it took 10 needlewomen eight weeks to apply the 1.7 million stitches needed to attach a linen backing to the flag. It took the equivalent of seven human years of labor to remove those stitches.

The American flag was originally based on the British Grand Union Flag, which had 13 alternating red and white stripes and a Union Jack in the upper left-hand corner, where our stars are located. With the signing of the Declaration of Independence and the start of the American Revolution, it became obvious to the young Continental Congress that the new democracy needed its own flag and not a copy of the British Grand Union. After all, the idea was to break away from the chains of England. The daunting task of designing our country's new flag went to the New Jersey delegate to the Second Continental Congress, Francis Hopkinson. Hopkinson happened to be friends with a woman named Betsy Ross and asked her to replace the Union Jack and in its place sew in a blue field with 13 white stars to represent each of the new states. It is also believed that George Washington offered his suggestions regarding the stars and representation of the new states. On June 14, 1777, the Continental Congress adopted this new design as the flag of the 13 United States.

During the Congress of 1818, two major events occurred. The Second Flag Resolution was enacted, which stated that the field of stripes would remain at 13 with a star being added for each state to join the Union, and it was decreed that July 4 would be the official "date of recognition" for stars to be added to the flag. On May 30, 1916,

13-Star American Shield said to have been used during the 1789 presidential inauguration of George Washington, 1789, approximately 2' 9-½" x 4' ½", $25,000-$30,000

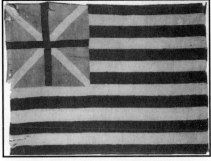

American Grand Union or Continental Flag, 1790–1810, approximately 1' 8" x 2' 3", $60,000-$75,000. This is the only known example from the late 18th to the early 19th century of the flag that represented the United States prior to its separation from England.

13-Star American Indian Peace Flag, 1850, approximately 1' 11" x 2' 8", $15,000-$18,000. To win the loyalty of Native American tribal chiefs, the federal government gave them flags with eagles in cantons. This peace flag is one of only five known examples.

President Woodrow Wilson established Flag Day, and President Harry S. Truman's 1949 signature on an Act of Congress designated June 14 as the official Flag Day.

Today, our flag, the American flag, is flying as high and proud as ever and has once again brought our country to "Rally Around the Flag."

13-Star American National Flag, 1861–1865

Hand-sewn single-appliquéd cotton muslin, approximately 3' 5" x 6' 10-$^7/_{16}$". Stars configured in unusual pattern that was first utilized during the Civil War. $6500-$7500

13-Star American National Flag Commemorating the Centennial Celebration of American Independence, 1876

Hand-sewn double-appliquéd cotton muslin, approximately 4' 4-$^7/_{16}$" x 6' 3". Stars configured in alternating rows of three and two. $2500-$3000

13-Star American National Flag Commemorating the Centennial Celebration of American Independence, 1876

Treadle machine–sewn double-appliquéd cotton muslin, approximately 8' 1-$^7/_{16}$" x 11' 4-$^7/_{16}$". Stars configured in a unique pattern of nine stars surrounding a square of four inner stars. $5000-$6000

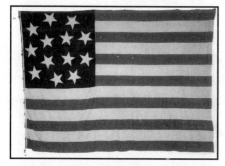

13-Star American National Flag commemorating the centennial celebration of American independence, 1876, $5000-$6000

Replica 15-Star, 15-Stripe American National Flag Made for the Centennial Celebration of American Independence, 1876

Hand-sewn double-appliquéd cotton muslin, approximately 4' 9" x 6' 8". Stars configured in staggered straight rows on a machine-sewn blue cotton canton. $2500-$3500

13-Star American National Flag commemorating the centennial celebration of American independence, 1876, $5000-$6000. Extremely rare size—only one other flag having this pattern known to exist.

17-Star American National Flag Commemorating Ohio Statehood on February 19, 1803, Made 1861–1865

Hand-sewn double-appliquéd eight-sided cotton muslin, approximately 3' 2-$^7/_{16}$" x 3' 7". Stars configured in a "global scatter" pattern on a cotton pattern. $12,500-$15,000

18-Star American National Flag Commemorating Louisiana Statehood on April 30, 1812, Made 1812–1816

Hand-sewn single-appliquéd, approximately 3' 11" x 8' 6". Stars configured in straight rows on a three-piece wool bunting canton. $18,000-$20,000
Only one of two known 18-star flags to have survived.

19-Star American National Flag Commemorating Indiana Statehood on December 11, 1816, Made 1861–1863

Hand-sewn double-appliquéd cotton muslin, approximately 8' 6" x 8' 7". Stars configured in a "double-wreath" pattern around a large central star representing Indiana. $3500-$4000

20-Star American National Flag Commemorating Mississippi Statehood on December 10, 1817, Made 1817–1818

Hand-sewn single-appliquéd cotton muslin, approximately 4' x 5' 7-$^7/_{16}$". Stars configured on a wool bunting canton with the vertical axis of each row of stars pointing upward or downward. $10,000-$13,000
Third official American National Flag.

24-Star American National Flag Commemorating Missouri Statehood on August 10, 1821, Made 1821–1836

Hand-sewn single-appliquéd cotton muslin, approximately 5' 9-$^7/_{16}$" x 10' 11". Stars configured in four straight rows of six with scatter to the vertical axis of each star. $8000-$10,000

25-Star American National Flag Commemorating Arkansas Statehood on June 15, 1836, Made 1821 and Updated 1836–1837

Hand-sewn double-appliquéd cotton muslin, approximately 9' 3" x 12' 4". Stars configured in five straight rows. $7500-$8500

28-Star American National Flag Commemorating Texas Statehood on December 29, 1845, Made 1845–1846

Hand-sewn cotton stripes and machine-sewn stars, approximately 2' 8" x 4' 2". Stars configured into the "Great Star" or "Great Luminary" pattern. $7500-$8500

29-Star Parade Flag, Mexican-American War

Coarse cotton material, approximately 7" x 10". Stars configured into the "Great Star" pattern. $140-$160

31-Star American National Flag, 1850–1858, thought to have been used in the 1860 campaign of Abraham Lincoln, approximately 5' 3" x 12' 8-⁷/₁₆", $10,000-$15,000

34-Star American National Flag Commemorating Kansas Statehood on January 29, 1861, Made 1861–1863

Hand-sewn double-appliquéd cotton muslin, approximately 2' 3" x 3' 7". "Plump Starfish" stars configured in the unique "Southern Cross" pattern commonly found on flags of the Confederacy. $45,000-$60,000

34-Star American National Presidential Campaign Flag, 1868

Paint-printed on linen with remnants of a paper label along the fly edge of both sides reading "Grant and Colefax," approximately 1' 10" x 2' 9-⁷/₁₆". $4000-$5000 Used during Ulysses S. Grant's presidential campaign of 1868.

35-Star American National Cavalry Guidon Flag Commemorating West Virginia Statehood on June 20, 1863, Made 1863–1864

Gilt-painted stars configured in a "double wreath" or "double medallion" pattern onto a silk canton, machine-sewn silk stripes, approximately 2' 2-⁷/₁₆" x 3' 3-⁷/₁₆". $15,000-$18,000

Patriotic Flag Handkerchiefs, American, 1864–1876 (one pair)

First flag: 36-Star American National Flag printed on a silk handkerchief to commemorate Nevada's admission into the Union on October 31, 1864. Second flag: 38-Star American National Flag printed on a silk handkerchief to commemorate independence from Great Britain. Each approximately 1' 7-⁷/₁₆" x 1' 7-⁷/₁₆". $800-$1000

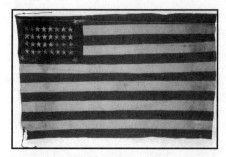

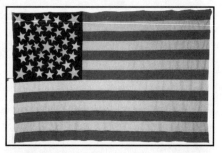

36-Star American National Flag commemorating Nevada statehood on October 31, 1864, made 1864–1867, approximately 5' 1-⁷/₁₆" x 8' 4", $6500-$7500

38-Star American National Flag commemorating Colorado statehood on August 1, 1876, made 1876–1889, approximately 7' 4" x 11' 5", rare, $4500-$5000

39- and 40-Star American National Flag Commemorating North and South Dakota Statehood, November 2, 1889, Made 1889

Hand-sewn cotton muslin with stars affixed to cotton canton, approximately 8' 3" x 9' 3-⁷/₁₆". The 13th stripe has a rare embroidered date of 1876 sewn into it. $12,500-$15,000

43-Star American National Flag Commemorating Idaho Statehood, July 3, 1890, Made 1890

Stars gilt-painted with maroon and mustard highlights in a "double medallion" or "double-wreath" pattern, approximately 4' 7" x 6' 3-⁷/₁₆". $12,500-$15,000

44-Star American National Flag Commemorating Wyoming Statehood on July 10, 1890, Made 1890–1896

Hand-sewn double-appliquéd cotton muslin, approximately 5' 6" x 8' 3". Stars configured in a notched pattern with some scatter to the vertical axis on each star. $2000-$2500

45-Star American National Parade Flag, 1918

Clamp-dyed parade flag printed on cotton, approximately 11" x 1' 2". $1200-$1500 Possibly belonged to a member of the Expeditionary Forces to carry as a "Bible" flag while serving in France during World War I.

48-Star Flag

Printed on heavy canvas-type material, approximately 5-³/₄" x 4-¹/₂", worn under the camouflage net on helmets. $90-$100 Used by Army infantry during Normandy Invasion, begun June 6, 1944.

American World War I Son-in-Service Banner, 1918
Vertical hanging satin banner of two blue machine-sewn stars on a white center rectangle surrounded by a field of red, approximately 4' 10" x 3'. $750-$950

United States Revenue Cutter Flag, 1860–1870
Treadle machine–sewn, canton and stripes are wool bunting with a double-appliquéd eagle with a shield on its breast surrounded by 13 stars on the canton, approximately 4' 7" x 7' 6". $3000-$4000
Only national flag having vertical stripes.

Folk Art

*F*olk art, sometimes referred to as *primitives*, is a very different and unique art form that actually has no specific period and is still designed and handcrafted by today's artists. Up until the 1920s, folk art was not given much attention, because of its unsophisticated style and the artists, whose talents had not been exposed to any type of academic training or schooling in the various art forms. Also, much of the folk art was crafted without any regard to size and scale and was therefore not considered artistic.

Because of their encouragement, Gertrude Vanderbilt Whitney and Abby Aldrich Rockefeller deserve a great deal of the credit for bringing folk art to the center of attention. The first major exhibit of folk art was held at the Whitney Studio Club, a gathering place for many artists, which was established by Whitney in New York City in 1924. This club later expanded and became the Whitney Museum of American Art. Rockefeller assisted in the establishment of the Museum of Modern Art in New York City and the Colonial Williamsburg restoration in Virginia, which has a museum (named in her honor) housing a large collection of folk art.

Another prominent individual who contributed greatly to the collection and enhancement of folk art was Herbert Waide Hemphill, Jr. His principle interests were art, theater, and poetry. In 1948, Hemphill studied fine arts from painter and folk art collector Stefan Hirsh. In 1956, Hemphill purchased a pair of cigar-store Indians, and from that point on he concentrated on American folk art. In 1961, Hemphill was one of the founders of the Museum of Early American Folk Arts (today the

American Folk Art Museum) in New York; three years later he resigned from the board of trustees to become the museum's first curator. Between 1986 and 1998 the Smithsonian American Art Museum acquired more than 500 works from Hemphill's collection. He bequeathed the balance of his collection to the museum with instructions to use the proceeds from its sale to establish the Herbert Waide Hemphill Jr. Folk Art Fund. The sale and auction was conducted by Slotin Folk Art Auctions, Buford, Georgia. A number of the patriotic folk art items referenced in this chapter were from the Herbert Waide Hemphill, Jr. Estate. I would like to thank Slotin Folk Art Auctions for their time and assistance. I would also like to thank Diana Douglas and Michael Ogle of American Garage, Van Nuys, California, for their contribution of both photographs and assistance with understanding the world of folk art.

The various types of folk art can be broken down into four categories:

1. Paintings accomplished by stencil, called *theorems.*
2. Drawings that depict unique penmanship skill, called *calligraphic.*
3. *Frakturs,* which are ornately designed documents recording births, baptisms, and marriages.
4. *Mourning pictures* in ink, watercolors, or embroidery to honor the death of someone close to the artist.

Today the collecting and study of folk art has become one of the most enjoyable and interesting areas of art for collectors and designers throughout the world.

American flag, Native American weaving, 24" x 29" (Hemphill Estate), $500

1976 Bicentennial
Map of the United States surrounded by American flags, oil on canvas, framed, 35" x 25", artist: Pappy Kitchens. $175

Abraham Lincoln Leaning on a Rail
Marker and crayon on cardboard, 11" x 13", in a tramp art frame, 19" x 21" (Hemphill Estate). $200

Abstract Statue of Liberty, 1989
Paint on paper, 14" x 22", artist: Charlie Lucas. $350

American Eagle
Hooked rug, 38" x 53" (Hemphill Estate). $1400

American Eagle and Stars Placemats
Pieced and quilted cloth placemats, which are blue with red stars and white American eagles, 19" x 16" (Hemphill Estate). $110

American Flag Pillow
Embroidered and hand-sewn, initials "Z A B" under (red, white, and blue) flag, 17" x 20" (Hemphill Estate). $25

American Flag Pillows (six pillows)
Largest 24" x 15", smallest 10" x 7" (Hemphill Estate). $140 (all six)

Angel with Bible and Statue of Liberty, 1991
Paint on board, 48" x 24", artist: R. A. Miller. $600

Banner, 1876
Patriotic banner for state of Maryland to celebrate the centennial (1776–1876). Gold shield on a red, white, and blue banner. Gold shield has a painting of a lady holding a sword with ships in the background. $2800
Banner was used in centennial parades.

Banner, 1876
Patriotic banner for State of Oregon to celebrate the centennial (1776–1876). Gold shield on a red, white, and blue banner. Gold shield has a painting of an Indian holding a bow standing next to a gold frame with a ship, eagle, and beaver in background. $2800
Banner was used in centennial parades.

Bicentennial Crocheted Throw Blankets (four blankets)
Red, white, and blue blankets (Hemphill Estate). $50

Broken Flag, 1972
Oil on canvas painting of broken American Flag, framed, 24" x 30", artist: Stephen Dudko (Vietnam veteran). $200

Casket Parade, 1972
Oil on canvas painting of a group of caskets draped with flags, framed, 36" x 48", artist: Stephen Dudko (Vietnam veteran). $275

Civil War Soldier, 1865
Carved oak man with shovel, 23" high (Hemphill Estate). $650

Dancing Uncle Sam, 1880

Hand-carved and painted wood Uncle Sam dancing figure. Arms jointed at shoulders and elbows, legs jointed at knees and ankles. Figure is extended by $1/4$" dowel rod, 40" long from back side, 12" high. $900-$1200

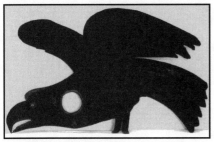

Eagle, painted metal sculpture, 24" x 14-$1/2$" (Hemphill Estate), $600

Dancing Uncle Sam, 1885

Wood and metal Uncle Sam figure extending from a stars and stripes post; dances on movable legs and arms when board is snapped, 15-$1/2$" x 28" x 8-$1/2$". $3000-$3500

Declaration of Independence

Colonial man reading the Declaration of Independence, pencil and ink on paper, 8" x 7", artist: Tom Tarrer. $35

"Eagle and Flag," 1975

Red border, red, white, and blue flag, eagle with stars and stripes in center, handspun wool, natural dyed, woven, Native American, internal frame, 29" x 44", artist: Grace Tony (Hemphill Estate). $800

Eagle Feeding Chick

Masonic painting depicting eagle feeding chicks with the word "Equality" underneath two hands shaking, oil on canvas and hand-painted frame, written "From Friendship Masonic Lodge," 4" x 36-$1/2$" (Hemphill Estate). $1000

George Washington, 1991, tempera on paper, 11" x 17", artist: Ike Morgan, $150

Early Uncle Sam Mailbox Post

Carved and painted wood, 22" x 59" (Hemphill Estate). $1000

Flag Landscape, 1972

Oil on canvas, framed, 48" x 36", artist: Stephen Dudko (Vietnam veteran). $250

George Washington Tattoo Flash

George Washington with American flags, ink on paper, framed, 12" x 9-$1/2$", artist: Bob Shaw (Hemphill Estate). $700

God Bless America, 1976

Large flag with people holding flags and marching, ink on paper, framed, 24" x 17", artist: Jack Savitsky. $800

Marquetry World War I patriotic colored wood inlay, 1918, 22-½" x 15-½" (Hemphill Estate), $2100. Illustrated on page 49 of *Twentieth-Century American Folk Art and Artists* (1974) by Herbert W. Hemphill, Jr. and Julia

"Jesus Is the Light of the World," 1988

Acrylic on canvas, red, white, and blue American flag with dark blue globe and cross in center reading "Jesus Is the Light of the World," 34-½" x 27", artist: B. F. Perkins. $900

Lady Liberty Andirons (for fireplace), 1900–1910

Two solid brass lady figures with red and white blouses and red, white, and blue skirts. $3500 (pair)

Left-Handed American Flag

Stars on left side of American flag, mixed-media on plastic, 24" x 18", artist: Baltimore Glassman. $250

Old Ironside Pry "Golden Eagle"

Blue background, paint on cardboard, framed, 10-½" x 15-½". $175

"The Regan Screw," 1989

Carved and painted wood Uncle Sam image sitting on screw, 8" x 8" x 20", artist: Ned Cartledge (Hemphill Estate). $1700

Pledge of Allegiance to the Flag, March 10, 1990, paint on board, 27-½" x 25", artist: B. F. Perkins, $900

Screaming Eagle with Steaming Battleship in Background, 1900

Pencil on paper, framed in beautiful wood frame with inlayed circles, 11-½" x 13-½", artist: Lee Carpender. $150

Rooster, 1890–1900, body is white, head and tail are red, $6500

Search for Utopia, 1981
American flag and children on magic carpet with bright sun in background. The magic carpet symbolizes the feeling for America as children, from sunrise to sunset; yarn fabric, hand-sewn and quilted, 21" x 26", artist: Mary Borkowski. $800

Statue of Liberty, 1984
Paint on tin, 27" high, artist: David Butler. $800

Statue of Liberty, July 4, 1989
Oil on canvas, 24" x 32", artist: B. F. Perkins. $1900

Statue of Liberty, 1900
Wood-carved Statue of Liberty made of pine, wrought-iron crown spokes, traces of black and yellow polychrome, 19-3/4" high. $2500-$3500

Statue of Liberty, paint on artist board, 8" x 10", artist: Bertha Halozan, $125

Statue of Liberty, February 18, 1991
Drawing depicts Statue of Liberty with good words about America, stars in background, oil on canvas, 18" x 24", artist: B. F. Perkins (Hemphill Estate). $1000

Statue of Liberty
Colored pencil on paper, framed, 12" x 8-1/2", artist: Dilmus Hall (Hemphill Estate). $300

Uncle Sam
Carved and painted wood, 14" high, artist: Ralph Buckwalter (Hemphill Estate). $850

Uncle Sam, October 1997
Painted cutout on base, 23" high, artist: Howard Finster. $350

Uncle Sam Card Tray Holder, 1976
Hand-carved and painted wood Uncle Sam figure holding a red card tray, painted on the inside with the American flag, eight stars, 13" high, 4" front to back, cardholder measures 4-1/2" x 5-1/4". $60-$80

Statue of Liberty, mud and paint on artist board, 23-½" x 48", artist: Jimmy Lee Sudduth, $500

Uncle Sam, Hitler Whimsical Wood Carving, 1942
Wood carving of Uncle Sam holding sledgehammer to hit head of Hitler on bell-ringing device, 15" high. $600-$700

Uncle Sam Papier-Mâché Head, 1890
Oversized head of Uncle Sam made of wire mesh and papier-mâché, 25" high. $450-$550
Head was used in Mardi Gras carnivals and parades.

Vision of George Washington
Paint on board, artist-made wood-burned frame, 48" x 41-½", artist: Howard Finster. $8500

Whirligig, 1935
Hand-carved wood figure of Uncle Sam mounted on wood block, 17-¼" x 5", with an arm spread of 13".
$175-$225

Woven Folk Art Frame, William Jennings Bryan, 1896 Campaign
Handcrafted frame consisting of a pair of cardboard sheets wrapped in strands of off-white and light pink thread woven to form exact geometric design of octagons, hexagons, squares, and triangles, 4-¼" x 1-¼", with photograph of Bryan in middle. $65-$75

"Yankee Battle Scene"
Oil on Masonite, framed, 51" x 33", artist: S. C. Baker (Hemphill Estate). $400

Stick toy, 1890-1910, wooden black male figure with white top hat and red legs (walks when a wooden stick is inserted in a hole behind the figure), $3200

You Go into the World, August 24, 1989
American flag with dark circle reading "Go into the Whole World and Preach the Gospel, Mark 16:15," paint on board, 32-½" x 16", artist: B. F. Perkins. $650

Young Abraham Lincoln, August 1985
Paint on thick cutout board, 77" high, artist: Howard Finster. $6000

Uncle Sam flagpole holder (right), 1918–1920, movable arms that swing out to hold flagpole, 60" high, $650-$750; Uncle Sam mailbox holder, 1918, cast-iron mailbox mounted on wooden swivel arms, 60" high, $750-$850

Uncle Sam stove top hat whirligig, red, white, and blue hat and metal blades (from industrial fan) turn in the wind, 60" x 25" (Hemphill Estate), $1000

Greeting Cards

The very first greeting card materialized in December 1843 when an Englishman, Henry Cole, decided he was too busy to write individual holiday greetings to his friends and acquaintances. To deal with his problem, Cole hired a well-known London artist, John Calcott Horsley, to design a card that could then be sent with his own personal holiday greeting instead of having to write individual messages. These early cards comprised various religious symbols that reflected the Christmas spirit. A number of the cards depicted such themes as the feeding of the poor, clothing the naked, and other important issues to people at that time.

The actual greeting card business, however, didn't start until 1860, when British publisher Charles Goodall & Son ventured into greeting cards by making cards to be used when visiting others. It was customary for middle- and upper-class people to leave a visiting card after making a formal visit to friends. Goodall then began to produce small cards, approximately 2" x 3" for visits at Christmas. The most sought-after cards are those that were manufactured between 1860 and 1890 by Goodall and its competitors: Marcus Ward & Company, De La Rue & Company, and Raphael Tuck & Company in England and L. Prang & Company in America. Prang was a German immigrant who began to produce Christmas cards in 1874 at his Roxbury, Massachusetts, printing plant. Eventually, other American card publishers, such as the Gibson Art Company, Rust Craft Greeting Cards, and Hallmark Cards, made their mark on the marketplace.

Traditionally, greeting cards have continued to capture the many significant historical growth, trends, and emotions of the United States. The first real wave of national patriotism by means of greeting cards became evident during the Spanish-American War and continued to grow to new levels with the advent of World War I. The Depression of the 1930s once again provided more subject matter that reflected the hard times of that era, such as Santa appearing with holes in his boots and pack. With the bombing of Pearl Harbor on December 7, 1941, holiday greeting cards transitioned from recognizing the Depression to recognizing World War II. Christmas cards with patriotic messages portraying images of Uncle Sam, the eagle, the Statue of Liberty, and American flags became high in demand.

This tradition continued with the Korean War and once again during the Vietnam War. Christmas trees appeared with stars and stripes and in nontraditional Christmas colors like red, white, and blue. After a time of peace, patriotic themes were once again introduced during the Persian Gulf conflict. And then, as America entered the 2001 holiday season, the tragedy of the September 11 terrorist attack on America occurred, which once again resulted in greeting cards reflecting the social needs and emotions of the American people. Hallmark Cards introduced four new patriotic holiday cards incorporating traditional holiday images such as wreaths and snowmen wrapped in red, white, and blue waving flags and including messages of peace, hope, and patriotism.

"Ahoy There, Merry Christmas," 1943
Soldier with Santa Claus on island, 4-$^1/_8$" x 5". $15–$20

Snowman waving American flag
with red shawl around neck,
Hallmark Cards, 2001, $20–$25

"Best Wishes to a Woman in the Service," 1943
Picture of American flag and flowers, 4-$^3/_4$" x 5-$^1/_2$".
$15–$20

"Christmas Greetings to a Fine Aviator," 1943
Pilot saluting in front of fighter plane, 4-$^3/_4$" x 5-$^3/_4$".
$15–$20

"Congratulations On Winning Your Wings,"
Hallmark Cards, 1943
P-47 fighter plane and flag, red ribbons on white
background, 5-$^3/_4$" x 5". $10–$15

"From One In The Service [eagle with wings in center] Who Loves You," Gibson Company, 1943
Easter card, white "V" symbol with roses, red, white, and blue, 8" x 10". $45-$55

"Good Luck to You in the Service," Hallmark Cards, 1942-1945, $10-$15

"A GIFT for Someone in the Service from All of US," 1943
U.S. flag on padded background, 5-³/₄" x 7". $15-$20

"Greetings," 1942
A picture of Santa Claus taking his cap off for Uncle Sam, 4-¹/₄" x 5-¹/₄".
$10-$15

"Greetings and Best Wishes to a Mighty Fine Soldier," 1944
Soldier in service cap, eagle over head, red, white, and blue 4-³/₄" x 5". $10-$15

"Happy Birthday to You in the Service," 1943
Eagle, "V," red, white, and blue, 5-¹/₄" x 6-¹/₄". $10-$15

"Merry Christmas—KEEP 'EM FLYING," Hallmark Cards, 1942–1945, $10-$15

"Hey Soldier, Bet 'Ya When You're Drilling, You Do Everything Just Right," 1942
Soldier with rifle, 5" x 5-⁷/₈". $10-$15

"Hi Soldier! I've Got Something Here You'll Like. Can't You Tell from My Expression?" 1943
Pretty young woman, 5" x 5-⁷/₈".
$10-$15

"Hope Merry Christmas Has Landed With You," 1943
Marine in dress blues, U.S. flag, gifts, 4-³/₄" x 5-³/₄". $15-$20

"I Want You," Hallmark Cards
Uncle Sam pointing with circle of stars in background, inside message "To Get Well! (Hope It's Soon)," red, white, and blue, 6-¹/₄" x 4-¹/₄". $5-$8

"A Letter to You in the Service," 1944
Young girl at table with the blue star banner in background, 4-³/₄" x 6". $10-$15

"Merry Christmas Sailor, Hope Everything Is Well With You," 1943
Red, white, and blue, 5" x 5-⁷/₈". $10-$15

"Merry Christmas," Hallmark Cards, 1942–1944, Uncle Sam top hat in red, white, and blue, $20-$25

"Merry Christmas Soldier!! Wish I could say I TOE-D YOU SO," 1943
Cartoon of woman writing to soldier in frame, 5" x 5-⁷/₈". $10-$15

"Remember Pearl Harbor," 1942
Uncle Sam rolling up left sleeve, red, white, and blue, 4-³/₄" x 5-³/₄". $20-$25

"Shoot Straight to a Happy Birthday," 1943
Soldier firing a machine gun, 5" x 6". $10-$15

"A sincere wish for a Merry American Christmas—and a Happy New Year"
Uncle Sam tipping his hat to Santa Claus and Santa saluting to Uncle Sam, 4-³/₄" x 5". $8-$10

"Something For Someone In The Service At Christmas Time," Hallmark Cards, 1942–1944, $15-$20

"To a Swell Guy in the Army, I'm Waving the Flag for You Soldier, And Wishing You Christmas Cheer," 1942
Pretty girl looking through "V" waving a U.S. flag, 4-³/₄" x 5-³/₄". $15-$20

"To a Young American, Merry Christmas," 1943
A picture of Uncle Sam driving a train, 4-¹/₂" x 5-³/₄". $10-$15

"To Someone in the Service," 1943
Picture of young sailor, soldier (reading letter), and flyer. $5-$10

"V for Victory," 1944
Red, white, and blue, 4-¹/₂" x 4-¹/₂". $10-$15

Christmas wreath with red, white, and blue ribbons, Hallmark Cards, 2001, $20-$25

"Victory Parade, Season's Greeting," Hanover Lee Company, 1945
Soldier, sailor, nurse, marine, and airman, 5" x 6". $10-$15

"We're Rootin' for You Soldier! Uncle Sam is pretty smart (In case you didn't know), He went and put You in the fight, To Hammer at the foe!" Cartoon character of Uncle Sam with his hand on the shoulder of a young soldier trying to look mean. The American flag rises as the card is opened, "Made in the U.S.A." 5-1/8" x 4-1/8". $8-$10

Magazines

*M*agazines have played a major role in keeping Americans informed of world events while providing reading entertainment and enjoyment since the early 1700s. During the 19th century, *Harper's* magazine was among the favorites for its political and literary essays. It wasn't until the 1900s that photojournalistic magazines such as *Life* magazine (1932) were introduced to the American public. This new magazine format had an immediate appeal and effect on readers who enjoyed viewing an instant idea of what was to follow in the magazine. While *Life* magazine led the way with this new format and approach, it wasn't long until other magazines, such as *The Saturday Evening Post, Collier's, Time,* and *Newsweek,* offered the same type of photojournalistic reporting. Since the beginning of our country, Uncle Sam has been a favorite subject of many magazines, but there were three magazines—*Harper's Weekly, Leslie's Weekly,* and *Puck*—that seemed to devote much time to the political side of Uncle Sam. This chapter will provide a sampling of the various covers from these three magazines.

As America entered World War II, this photojournalistic approach became an immediate medium from which to bring about an awakening of patriotism in our country in support of the war effort. The history and legacy that these magazines have left for future generations can be considered as one of the most graphic and detailed chronological documentation of events of World War II. One of the most ambitious magazine campaigns that inspired America as the nation entered the war was an undertaking by approximately 500 magazines to feature an American flag on the cover of their Fourth of July, 1942 issue. Along with the depiction of the flag, about half of these magazines included the slogan "United We Stand." This idea came from Paul MacNamara, a publicist for Hearst magazines, and was strongly supported by Secretary of the Treasury Henry M. Morgenthau, Jr.

While this chapter lists a number of these magazines with photographs, a recently published book titled *United We Stand,* by Peter Gwillim Kreitler, June 2001, features more than 100 of the most striking covers from this campaign. His collection began when he received one of the covers, which was published the same month and year of his birth, as a gift. As with most collectors, the passion began and the rest is history. Since this campaign was so important in helping to restore a passion for the war and supporting the young war bonds effort, it was decided by the Smithsonian to provide the American public with a unique opportunity to view a very special page of history. With a gathering reminiscent of World War II, the Smithsonian National Museum of American History featured an exhibition of Kreitler's magazines called "July 1942: United We Stand," which ran through October 2002. I would like to thank Peter, who, with his wealth of knowledge, helped provide information for this book.

Adventure, June 1943
"Six Weeks, South of Texas," Leslie T. White. Cover depicts U.S. Army solider holding rifle and fighting. $10-$15

Adventure, October 1944
"The End of Jingle Bill," Thomson Burtis. Cover depicts U.S. soldier trying to decide whether to play dice with local island native helping U.S. Army. $10-$15

Elks magazine, July 1942, woman soldier raising American flag, $15-$20

The American Legion Magazine, January 1941
"All for one, one for all." Cover depicts Uncle Sam rolling up his sleeves in front of factory workers. Artist: J. W. Schlaikjer. $35-$40

The American Legion Magazine, July 1942
U.S. flag with Navy ships and fighter planes. $15-$20

Argosy, America's Oldest All-Fiction Magazine, July 1943
"Guns for Mr. Burr," Clifford Dowdey. Cover depicts soldiers landing on beach and firing machine guns. $15-$20

Collier's, February 14, 1942

"Stuka! New Air Fighters Menace You," W. B. Courtney. Cover depicts images of Hitler, Mussolini, and Hirohito. $35-$45

Collier's, July 25, 1942

"Four Fliers from Midway," Frank D. Morris. Cover depicts cartoon picture of monkey with image of a Japanese soldier pulling Hitler with image of monkey in cart. $45-$55

Collier's, January 29, 1944

"What I Saw in Russia," Donald Nelson. Cover depicts U.S. Army soldier holding tommy gun on prisoners. $15-$20

Everywoman's magazine, July 1943, small girl holding American flag, $10-$15

Collier's, July 14, 1945

"MacArthur: The Story of a Great American Soldier." Cover depicts female entertainer wearing camp show uniform. $15-$20

The Country Gentlemen, June 16, 1917

Cover depicts Uncle Sam standing with U.S. Army soldier on one side and farmer saluting on other side. Quote at bottom of magazine: "Upon the farmers of this country, therefore in large measure, rest the fate of the war and the fate of the nations" (President Wilson). Artist: Herbert Johnson. $75-$85

The Country Gentlemen, October 1936

Cover depicts Uncle Sam with hat off, scratching his head, holding road sign reading "Prosperity," as he looks at the following road signs: "New Deal," "Liberty," "Depression," "Inflation," and "Opportunity." Artist: Frank Lea. $50-$60

The Etude, Presser Musical Magazine, July 1917

Cover depicts Uncle Sam with sword and playing trumpet. Artist: E. H. Kreps. $40-$45

Fortune, May 1935

Uncle Sam on stilts in the circus. $35-$45

Fortune, July 1942

U.S. flag flying outside window with eagle and rifle inside by window. $20-$25

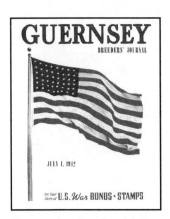

Guernsey, American flag, July 1, 1942, $10-$15

Harpers, July 1942
"Who's Going to Be Drafted?" Cover depicts American flag. $10-$15

Hollywood, September 1941
Cover depicts photograph of actor Tyrone Power with his pilot helmet and leather bomber jacket. $75-$100

The Home, a Tower Magazine, July 1932
Cover depicts a little boy marching and holding the American flag. Artist: Charles Twelvetrees. $20-$25

Jack and Jill, July 1944
Cover depicts many cartoon-type Uncle Sams carrying the following signs: "5th War Loan Drive," "Complete Your Stamp Book," "Buy War Stamps," and "Get A Bond." Artist: Stella May Dacosta. $25-$30

Knit for Defense, 1941
Cover depicts U.S. Army soldier with new knit sweater. $8-$10

Liberty, February 13, 1932
"Our Appalling Crisis—What Would Lincoln Do?" Cover depicts Abraham Lincoln pointing finger with pieces of paper reading "Unemployment, Farm Relief, and Prohibition. Artist: James Montgomery Flagg. $60-$75

Liberty, July 10, 1943, American flag, $5-$10

Liberty, November 7, 1936
"Election 1936." Cover depicts Uncle Sam with paintbrush, holding figures of elephant and donkey. Artist: Scott Evans. $50-$70

Liberty, July 11, 1942
"United We Stand" and "How We Can Lick the U-Boat Menace." Cover depicts flying American flag. $15-$20

Liberty, April 24, 1943
Cover depicts soldier fighting, with fighter planes in background. $10-$15

Liberty, January 15, 1944
Cover depicts General George C. Kenney. $5-$10

Life & Health, April 1942, mom showing American flag to young son, $10-$15

Life, July 6, 1942
"United We Stand." Cover depicts flying American flag. $20-$25

Life, September 17, 1945
Cover depicts photograph of General MacArthur, "Commander Of Japan." $25-$35

Life, September 24, 1945
Cover depicts photograph of Colonel Jimmy Stewart. $25-$30

Linens & Domestics, July 19, 1942
Illustration of American flag with marching U.S. Army soldier, marine, sailor, and nurse. Beneath flag is the "Pledge of Allegiance." $15-$20

Look, June 1, 1943
Cover depicts photograph of General George Patton. $25-$35

Milestones, July 1917
"The Conscript." Cover depicts Uncle Sam with rolled-up sleeves, flexing his muscles, with fists clenched. Artist: Clyde Forsythe. $90-$100

Modern Industry, June 15, 1942
"United We Stand." Cover depicts U.S. marine with factory workers standing in front of large American flag. $10-$15

National Geographic, July 1942
"Buy U.S. War Savings Bonds and Stamps." Cover depicts American flag. $15-$20

New England Homestead, January 2, 1897
"Happy New Year Prosperity." Uncle Sam holding old suit with caption "Uncle Sam's New Suit and what He Hopes to Secure From It." $200-$250

Newsweek, July 6, 1942
"United We Stand" and "Buy War Bonds And Stamps For Victory." Cover depicts flying American flag. $15-$20

Radio News, July 1943, soldier in the field talking on radio, $10-$15

The New Yorker, July 3, 1989
Cover depicts cartoon character of Uncle Sam setting off fireworks with Statue of Liberty taking his picture. Artist: Lee Lorenz. $10-$15

Opportunity, The New Declaration of Independence, Salesmanship, July 1935
Uncle Sam standing watch over salesmen. $20-$30

Our Army, July 1942
Cover depicts flying American flag. $10-$15

Our Navy, July 1942
"United We Stand." Cover depicts flying American flag. $10-$15

Parents Magazine Press, 1942
"How BOYS and GIRLS Can Help WIN THE WAR" all told in full-color comics. Cover depicts Uncle Sam saying "I'm counting on both of YOU!" to happy boy and girl. $20-$25

Popular Mechanics Magazine, August 1942
"Alloys for the Allies, United We Stand, Buy United States War Savings Bonds and Stamps," with U.S. flag surrounded by tanks, trucks, and soldiers. $15-$20

The Saturday Evening Post, July 1, 1944, depiction of Norman Rockwell painting "Soldier Looking at War Bond." $15-$20

Reader's Digest, July 1942
Cover depicts flying American flag. $10-$15

The Saturday Evening Post, July 4, 1936
"Flight." Uncle Sam holding the wheel and steering the ship with American eagle in background. Artist: J. C. Leyendecker. $75-$85

Screen Guide, August 1942
Cover depicts American flag with the "Service Man's Sweetheart," Betty Grable. $10-$15

Time, July 25, 1969
"Man On The Moon." Cover depicts astronaut on moon holding American flag. $10-$15

Town & Country, July, 1942
"Buy War Bonds And Stamps." Cover depicts illustration of many American flags.
$10-$15

"The Open Road for Boys," July 1942, three young men marching and holding American flag, $10-$15

Truth, The American Weekly, July 20, 1898
"The Foremost Star." Illustration of a smiling Uncle Sam. $40-$60

U.S. Army Recruiting and Career Counseling Journal, September 1974
Uncle Sam pointing finger saying "I Want QUALITY." Artist: James Montgomery Flagg. $15-$20

What's New, May 1942
"Don't let that SHADOW touch them—War Bonds." Cover depicts three young children playing, holding U.S. flags and toy planes. $20-$25

Woman's Day, July 1944
Hand holding $100 savings bond. $15-$20

Harper's Weekly

Beginning in the 1850s to the turn of the century, *Harper's Weekly* was considered the most popular illustrated periodical of its time. Unlike some of the other magazines of that era, *Harper's* utilized wood-block illustrations by some of the best 19th-century American illustrators.

"General Orders," September 21, 1872
Uncle Sam standing at attention with rifle next to American flag. $50-$60

"Keeping The Bench Above Suspicion Of Dishonest Money," March 10, 1881
Uncle Sam sitting on bench reading "U.S. Supreme Bench." $15-$20

"The First Step Toward National Bankruptcy," February 16, 1878
Uncle Sam with foot caught in steel trap. $60-$70

"The Minuteman, Fixed By The Spirit of '76," April 1, 1876
Uncle Sam standing with rifle in hand. $90-$100

"New York and New Orleans, No North, No South, But The Union,"
March 19, 1881
Picture of Northern and Southern Civil War officers shaking hands with Uncle
Sam in the background. $90–$100

Leslie's Weekly

Leslie's Weekly magazine, one of the best illustrated periodicals of the late 19th century, used the artwork of some of the most renowned illustrators of the period, with
the full-color artwork being the most appealing.

"Come Across," May 18, 1918
Uncle Sam with nurse in front of huge red cross. $65–$75

"I Ought To Be Thankful, Peace With All The World, Bumper Crops, Money To
Loan," November 25, 1915
Uncle Sam having Thanksgiving dinner. $45–$60

"On To Cuba! Remember The Maine," May 5, 1898
Uncle Sam standing next to American soldier. $75–$90

"Rally Round The Flag, Boys!" May 26, 1898
Uncle Sam standing on steps, holding American flag, surrounded by Teddy
Roosevelt's Rough Riders. $45–$60

"Remember The Maine," April 28, 1898
Uncle Sam looking mad, holding American flag. $75–$90

"Uncle Sam, Spanish Justice and Honor Be Darned," April 14, 1898
Uncle Sam looking mean and serious, holding rifle. $45–$60

"U.S.A.," January 5, 1918
Picture of Uncle Sam with rifle and bayonet, riding in car driven by Miss Liberty.
$60–$75

"Watchful Waiting," April 23, 1914
Uncle Sam at grinding wheel sharpening sword. $45–$60

"What Are You Doing For Preparedness," July 6, 1916
Uncle Sam pointing to reader. This was the first appearance of James Montgomery
Flagg's "I Want You" image and caption, which was later to be used on the famous
recruiting poster. $250–$300

Puck Magazine Covers

Puck magazine covers are among the most unique and well-illustrated covers by some of the best artists of the 19th century, with the Uncle Sam *Puck* covers being the most desirable among collectors.

"The Best Remedy—'I Guess A Change Of Operators Is Wanted Here,'"
February 2, 1881
Uncle Sam throwing telegraph operators out of the office. $100-$125

"The Canal Situation," December 11, 1901
Uncle Sam with British gentlemen making sign that reads " Nicaragua Canal Treaty."
$140-$160

"Out Of The Silver Flood!" September 13, 1893
Uncle Sam pulling himself and Miss Liberty out of water with rope looking at sign that reads "Repeal Of The Senate Law By The 53rd Congress." $100-$125

"A Pretty Dish To Set Before The Nation," August 4, 1886
Uncle Sam surrounded by two cooks in front of a bowl that reads "Legislation Mush—49th Congress." $125-$140

"Shipwrecked Patriotism," February 22, 1882
Uncle Sam on log at sea carrying flag reading "Trade Issues." $125-$150

"The Task of Diogenes Not In It, Uncle Sam Looking For A Statesmen In The United States Senate," February 1, 1893
Uncle Sam with lantern looking into Senate chambers. $125-$150

"What's in it, – Tariff Bill – That's One Of Those Things Which No Fellow Can Find Out" March 21, 1883
Uncle Sam at lunch table with waiter bringing plate with big sausage that reads "Tariff Bill." $100-$125

Matchbook Covers

The following article was contributed by Bill Retskin (founder of the American Matchcover Collecting Club) who also publishes the *Front Striker Bulletin* and holds postal and online auctions. Bill, with a personal collection that numbers approximately 750,000 items, is considered a knowledgeable expert in the field of matchcover collecting. I want to thank Bill for taking the time to give us an insight into the hobby and history of matchcover collecting.

The first book matches were made in 1892 and were credited to Joshua Pusey, a Philadelphia patent attorney. In 1945, the Diamond Match Company celebrated the fiftieth anniversary of buying Pusey's patent, which began the commercial production of book matches. The earliest known advertising on book matches was created in 1896 with widespread distribution, compliments of the Mendelssohn Opera Company. The only surviving example of an ad from this early commercial pursuit reads as follows: "A cyclone of fun, powerful caste, pretty girls, handsome ward-robe, get seats early." On the front of the cover was a pasted-on photograph of the star of this comic organization, Thomas Lowden, a trombonist who was immortalized with the edict "America's Youngest Operatic Comedian."

As was true for many industries, the match industry took a hard hit as a result of the Great Depression. Advertising and discretionary expenditures were reduced among the traditional big business matchbook buyers. As a means of combating this problem, the Diamond Match Company created matchbooks that would be sold directly to the public. These matchbooks featured sports, movie, and nightlife personalities.

Several dozen sets highlighted local interest in such series as souvenir and education. Prior to the period of the Great Depression, this innovative sales idea had never been attempted on a large-scale national basis.

With the onset of World War II, advertising with matchbooks was about to change. As early as 1939, the Diamond Match Company as well as several other large American matchbook companies began to gear up production for things to come. Following the tragedy of the bombing of Pearl Harbor on December 7, 1941, most matchbook companies dedicated a substantial portion of their sales and production activity toward patriotic themes. The U.S. government became their biggest buyer, producing hundreds of different patriotic themes and slogans to keep up with the orders for millions of matchbooks.

During World War II, however, the Office of Price Administration (OPA) insisted that a free book of matches be given away with every pack of cigarettes. The OPA viewed this practice as mandatory, and regulations ensured continued free matchbooks with cigarette purchases. Free matchbooks had now become a mainstay and were soon taken for granted. The thinking was that since the price of a matchbook hadn't realized an increase in 50 years, why should the vendors complain.

By 1945, a staggering two and a half trillion (2,500,000,000,000) matches had been manufactured in the United States alone. Based on the figure of 20 matches per book, that equals 125 billion matchbooks. Since 1945, the figures have increased more than 100 times worldwide.

Mike Prero, editor of the Rathkamp Matchbook Society (RMS) bimonthly bulletin online at www.matchcover.org, and Richard Greene, both knowledgeable experts, offer these tips for maintaining matchcovers in top condition:

1. Be careful not to deface covers. They should never be stapled, glued, or cut.
2. Never write on the outside of covers. If you do have to make any marks, only use light pencil on the inside.
3. Don't wrap covers tightly in rubber-banded stacks. Don't store them in damp areas or areas where they will be directly exposed to sunlight for extended periods.
4. If the striker has been cut off, the matchcover is called a "bobtail" and is virtually worthless.

"All Out for Victory," 1941–1945
Ohio Match Company, 1-$^3/_8$" x 4-$^3/_8$". $3-$5

"All Service Men Welcomed, Everything Free," 1941–1945
Masonic Service Center. $7-$10

"Americans Will Always Fight for Liberty," 1943
American Sanitary Products Company. $7-$10

Army-Navy Pendant Flag, 1944
Ehrhardt Tool and Machine Company, St. Louis Missouri. $8-$13

Avenger, Torpedo Bomber, Carries a Full Size Torpedo Internally, 1941–1945
Bond Bread. $5-$8

"Be Proud That You Are an AMER-I-CAN" (American Flag Shield), 1941–1945
Macha Studio, Chicago, Illinois. $10-$12

Buccaneer, with Shipboard Fighter Bomber, 1941–1945
Bond Bread. $6-$12

"Buy Bonds in Victory Window," 1941–1945
Boston Store. $4-$7

"Buy U.S. War Stamps and Bonds Regularly," 1941–1945
3-Stars. $3-$6

"Buy War Bonds & Stamps," 1942–1945
Tiny's Men's Shop, 207 South Palafox Street, Pensacola, Florida. $5-$7

"Buy War Bonds," 1941–1945
"Quality Never Changes," 7UP, Joyce Seven Up Bottling Company, New Rochelle,
New York. $12-$17

"Buy War Bonds Now," 1942–1944
RX Matchless Resiliency, "The World's Finest Super Mileage Tire." $5-$7

"Buy War Savings Certificates Regularly," 1943–1945
"Pull for Victory" with bird and worm. $7-$10

"Careless Lips Can Sink Ships," 1941–1945
Match Corp. of America, 1-³/₈" x 4-³/₈". $4-$5

**"Careless Lips," "God Bless America," "Smash the Axis," "Step on It," "Total
Eclipse," "We Shall Not Fail Her" (set two of six)**
Match Corp. of America. $5-$8

"Cherish Your Liberty & Grant It to Others," 1941–1945
3-Star Banner. $10-$12

"Corssair, the World's Fastest Ship Board Fighter," 1941–1945
Bond Bread. $4-$10

"Defend America," Match Corp. of America, 1941–1945, airplane, tank, ship, 1-³⁄₈" x 4-³⁄₈", $3-$5

**"Damn the Torpedoes—Full Speed Ahead,"
1941–1945**
General Match Company, 1-³⁄₈" x 4-³⁄₈".
$10-$12

**"Dauntless, with Scout-Dive Bomber Has Been
in Battles of Midway and Coral Sea," 1941–1945**
Bond Bread. $6-$10

**"Defend Yourself, 'Save with Safety,' Remember
Pearl Harbor, Buy War Stamps"**
Reese Drugs. $12-$17

"For Defense, Buy United States Savings Bonds and Stamps with Minuteman"
Stewart & Company, Maryland. $5-$8

"For Protection of Our Nation, Buy Bonds," 1941–1945
Match Corp. of America, 1-³⁄₈" x 4-³⁄₈". $3-$5

"For Victory, Buy United States War Savings Bonds and Stamps," 1941–1945 Bromo-Seltzer Fast Headache Relief, $4-$5

"For the Nation, Hold That Line, Hurry Back"
(soldiers marching), 1942–1943
Leo's Smoke Shop, San Jose, California. $8-$9

"For Victory, Let's Go U.S.A., Keep 'em Rolling"
(with tank), 1941–1945
Brahaney's, 325 High Street, Buffalo, New
York. $5-$8

"Free to Service Men" (three servicemen walking),
1942–1945
American Theatre Wing, Stage Door Canteen of
Cleveland. $7-$10

General Douglas MacArthur Color Set of Five, "Give 'em Both Barrels, Buy War Bonds and Stamps"
Arrow Match Company. $30-$45

General MacArthur, 1941–1945
Arrow Match Company, 1-³/₈" x 4-³/₈". $8-$10

"God Bless America, We Are Proud to Be American," 1941–1945
Eureka Lodge, 626 Church Street. $6-$9

"I am Proud that I am an American!"
1942–1945, American flag, $5-$7

"God Bless America, We Are Proud to Be American," 1942–1945
Will Rogers Motor Court, on U.S. Highway 66, Tulsa, Oklahoma. $8-$12

"God Bless America" (with Liberty Bell), 1941–1945
Bob's Food Market, York, Pennsylvania. $6-$9

"God Save America" (American flag banner), 1941–1945
With Morse & Wreath. $9-$15

"Keep Them Flying," 1941–1945, $4-$7

"I Shall Return" (crossed Philippine/U.S. flag, General Douglas MacArthur with signature and "I Shall Return")
Universal Match Corporation U.S.A. $75-$100

"Insure Your Share in America, Buy War Stamps & Bonds Today," 1942
National Hotel Week, June 1-7, 1942. $5-$8

"Invest in the U.S.A., Buy War Bonds, Keep 'em Flying," 1941–1945
Jersey Match Company. $5-$8

"Keep Democracy from Dying," 1941–1945
Match Corp. of America, 1-³/₈" x 4-³/₈". $4-$5

"Let's Go U.S.A.," 1943–1945, soldiers marching with bomber and Stars and Stripes shield, $4-$6

"Keep 'em Rolling," 1941–1945
Match Corp. of America, 1-³/₈" x 4-³/₈". $4-$5

"Keep Smiling, V for Victory," 1941–1945
Ohio Match Company, 1-³/₈" x 4-³/₈". $4-$5

"Know Your Endorsers, Don't Cash Checks for Strangers Without Identification" (Uncle Sam waving finger), 1942–1944
The U.S. Secret Service. $5-$8

"Know Your Money, Uncle Sam & the United States Secret Service"
Kendall's Kozy Korner, The Dalles, Oregon. $8-$13

"Let's All Be Americans Now," 1942–1944
Langtry Master-Glo Finish with Buffalo. $6-$9

"Let's All Help to Keep 'em Fighting" (with plane gunner), 1941–1945
Art Medal Manufacturing Company. $7-$10

"Let's Go! U.S.A. Keep 'em Flying," 1941–1945
Tek Brush, Johnson & Johnson, Your Choice. $4-$7

"O-K America, Let's Go," Diamond Match Company, 1941–1945, 1-³/₈" x 4-³/₈", $3-$5

"The More Bonds You Buy, the More Planes Will Fly," 1941–1945
The Chocolate Bar, Choice Drinks, Best Entertainment. $5-$7

"Own a Share in America with Minuteman Buy War Bonds"
"Step on It! World to Crush the Axis." $3-$5

"Preserve Freedom Not Slavery," 1941–1945
Arrow Match Company, 1-³/₈" x 4-³/₈". $4-$5

"Put Your Savings into War Bonds," 1941–1945
Ohio Match Company, 1-³/₈" x 4-³/₈". $3-$5

"Remember Pearl Harbor," 1941–1945
General Match Company, 1-³/₈" x 4-³/₈". $10-$15

"Salute Our Army Air Base, Santa Ana, California," 1941–1945
Diamond Match Company, 1-³/₈" x 4-³/₈". $3-$4

"United We Stand!" with Uncle
Sam, 1941–1945, $4-$7

"Season's Greeting with Uncle Sam, Victory in '43"
$5-$8

"Service Men's Only Retreat"
USO Club, Hyannis, Massachusetts, USO
logo. $5-$7

"Strike 'em Dead, Remember Pearl Harbor," 1941
$10-$12

"These Colors Never Run," 1941–1945
Williams Café, Scranton, Iowa. $4-$7

"United We Stand," 1941–1945
National Press Company, 1-³/₈" x 4-³/₈". $3-$5

U.S. Army & Navy Campaign Ribbons (four ribbons with names)
New Jersey Bell Telephone Company. $12-$18

"V for Victory" (back), "Buy War Saving Bonds
and Stamps" (front), 1943–1945, $5-$8

"V for Victory, V, Minuteman & Buy
Bonds," 1941–1945
$5-$8

"We Must Win! Buy More War
Bonds, Stamps" (with plane), "Our
Duty First, Buy More War Bonds,
Stamps" (with eagle)
$3-$5

"We're Proud of It!" (Army-Navy flag), 1943–1945
Eaton Metal Products, Albuquerque, Billings, Denver, Omaha. $6-$9

Women's Ambulance & Defense Corps of America
$3-$6

"Write Your Soldier a Letter Today!" (with soldier and rifle), 1941–1945
Jones Milk, "Guarding Your Health." $5-$8

V for Victory with Minuteman,
1941–1945, $5-$8

"You Are Working to Win," 1941–1945
Universal Match Company, 1-³/₈" x 4-³/₈". $3-$5

"Your Scrap Is Vital for Defense," 1941–1945
Abrams & Sons. $5-$7

Movie Posters—
War Themes

When you were growing up and walked by a movie theater, what was the first thing that caught your attention? The movie poster, right? Now that you are all grown up, what catches your attention when you walk by a movie theater? The movie poster, right? The movie industry and that poster outside the theater have been together since the movie poster made its debut in 1890. These colorful posters, which have awakened our patriotic passions on more than one occasion, often with very few words, deliver a message to the public that is understood in an instant. Posters depicting fighting marines, fighter pilots, Navy destroyers, Army tanks, American flags, and Uncle Sam, with John Wayne featured in many of the films, brought World War II directly to the home front and captured the hearts of every American. While World War II was predominantly the main theme, the movie studios were quick to also include other war themes such as the Revolutionary War, Civil War, and World War I. These posters also promoted the purchase of war bonds and stamps, scrap metal drives, and conservation efforts.

How did this all start? Actually, a young French artist and lithographer, Jules Cheret, is considered by the advertising industry to be the architect of the modern poster and is credited with the creation of the movie poster. In 1890, Cheret created a lithograph for a short film titled *Projections Artistiques* that depicted a young lady holding a placard with the time of the shows—and the rest is history. A little-known fact is that Thomas Edison was responsible for setting the standard size for a movie poster, which is 27" x 41" and was designed to be displayed in glass cases outside and inside the theaters.

As our country entered World War II, the movie studios and their many stars put production in high gear, creating and promoting a feverish climate of patriotism as never seen before in the movie industry. The studios, in fact, temporarily lost many of their stars (such as Clark Gable and Jimmy Stewart) to the real war. But the stars who didn't enlist made their contribution to the war effort by appearing in numerous films. Soon, war movies became the driving force in the industry, causing them to be one of the most watched type of movie since the beginning of film and resulting in more films being produced about World War II than any other war in history. These films were also large supporters of war bonds, with fund-raisers being held before the movie, during intermission, and after the movie.

Today, that colorful, bright, and exciting movie poster is still outside your favorite theater telling passersby to "Come on in and enjoy the movie."

Abraham Lincoln, 1924 (Civil War)
Walter Huston, United Artists Picture, window card 14" x 22". $300–$400

A Bridge Too Far, 1977 (World War II)
Michael Caine and Sean Connery, United Artists, 27" x 41". $175–$250

Action in the North Atlantic, 1943 (World War II)
Humphrey Bogart and Raymond Massey, U.S. War Department, 27" x 41". $300–$400

All Quiet on the Western Front, 1930 (World War I)
Universal Pictures, 27" x 41". $300–$400

America, 1924 The Midnight Ride of Paul Revere (Revolutionary War)
Produced by D. W. Griffith, window card, 14" x 22". $700–$1000

Armored Attack, 1943 (World War II)
John Garfield and Gig Young, Warner Brothers, 28" x 22". $75–$100

Arms and the Woman, 1944 (World War II)
Edward G. Robinson and Ruth Warrick, Columbia, 14" x 22". $100–$150

At Dawn We Die, 1942 (World War II)
Jon Clements and Hugh Sinclair, British, 14" x 36". $100–$150

Back to Bataan, 1945 (World War II)
John Wayne and Anthony Quinn, RKP, 41" x 81". $700-$800

Battleground, 1949 (World War II)
Van Johnson and Ricardo Montalban, MGM, 27" x 41". $100-$125

Battle of the Bulge, 1965 (World War II)
Henry Fonda and Robert Ryan, Warner Brothers, 27" x 41". $250-$350

The Birth of a Nation, 1915 (Civil War)
Produced by D. W. Griffith, 27" x 41". $800-$1000

The Blue Max, 1966 (World War I)
George Peppard and James Mason, 20th Century Fox, 27" x 41". $50-$75

The Bridge on the River Kwai, 1957 (World War II)
William Holden, Alec Guinness, and Jack Hawkins, Columbia, 27" x 41". $300-$400

The Bugle Sounds, 1941 (World War II)
Wallace Berry, Marjorie Main, and Lewis Stone, MGM, 27" x 41". $150-$200

Captains of the Clouds, 1942 (World War II)
James Cagney and Dennis Morgan, U.S. War Department, 27" x 41". $300-$400

Casablanca, 1942 (World War II)
Humphrey Bogart and Ingrid Bergman, U.S. War Department, 41" x 81".
$1300-$1500

Commandos Strike at Dawn, 1942 (World War II)
Paul Muni and Anna Lee, a Columbia Picture, 27" x 41". $250-$350

Crash Dive, 1943 (World War II)
Tyrone Power and Dana Andrews, 20th Century Fox, 14" x 36". $300-$400

The Dawn Patrol, 1930 (World War I)
Douglas Fairbanks, Jr., First National & Vitaphone Picture, 27" x 41". $100-$125

Days of Glory, 1944 (World War II)
Gregory Peck and Tamara Toumanova, RKO, 27" x 41". $75-$100

The Desert Rats, 1953 (World War II)
Richard Burton and James Mason, 20th Century Fox. $200-$300

Desert Victory, **1944 (World War II)**
British Army/RAF Documentation, 20th Century Fox, 27" x 41". $200-$400

Desperate Journey, **1942 (World War II)**
Errol Flynn and Ronald Reagan, U.S. War Department, 28" x 22". $300-$400

Destination Tokyo, **1943 (World War II)**
Cary Grant and John Garfield, U.S. War Department, 27" x 41". $300-$400

Destroyer, **1943 (World War II)**
Edward G. Robinson and Glenn Ford, Columbia, 14" x 36". $150-$200

Devil Dogs of the Air, **1935 (World War I)**
James Cagney and Pat O'Brien, Warner Brothers, window card 14" x 22". $100-$125

The Eagle Has Landed, **1976 (World War II)**
Michael Caine and Robert Duvall, Columbia Pictures, 27" x 41". $75-$125

Eagle Squadron, **1942 (World War II)**
Robert Stack and Diana Barrymore, Universal, 14" x 36". $75-$100

A Farewell to Arms, **1932 (World War I)**
Gary Cooper and Helen Hayes, Paramount Pictures, 27" x 41". $250-$350

The Fighting Seebees, **1944 (World War II)**
John Wayne and Dennis O'Keefe, Republic, 27" x 41". $550-$650

Flying Leathernecks, **1951 (World War II)**
John Wayne and Robert Ryan, RKO Radio, 27" x 41". $350-$450

Flying Tigers, **1942 (World War II)**
John Wayne and Anna Lee, Republic, 27" x 41". $800-$900

God Is My Co-Pilot, **1945 (World War II)**
Dennis Morgan and Dane Clark, U.S. War Department, 27" x 41". $200-$300

The Great Escape, **1963 (World War II)**
Steve McQueen and James Garner, United Artists, 27" x 41". $300-$400

Guadalcanal Diary, **1943 (World War II)**
Preston Foster, Lloyd Nolan, William Bendix, Richard Conte, and Anthony
Quinn, 20th Century Fox, 27" x 41". $550-$650

Gung Ho! 1943 (World War II)
Randolph Scott and Alan Curtis, Universal, 27" x 41". $300-$400

A Guy Named Joe, 1943 (World War II)
Spencer Tracy and Irene Dunne, MGM Picture, 27" x 41". $150-$200

Halls of Montezuma, 1951 (World War II)
Richard Widmark and Jack Palance, 20th Century Fox, 27" x 41". $300-$400

Heroes All, 1918 (World War I)
Released by Imperial Distributing Corporation, New York, 27" x 41". $200-$300

The Immortal Sergeant, 1943 (World War II)
Henry Fonda and Maureen O'Hara, 20th Century Fox, 27" x 41". $300-$400

International Squadron, 1941 (World War II)
Ronald Reagan and Julie Bishop, U.S. War Department, 28" x 22". $250-$300

I Wanted Wings, 1941 (World War II)
Ray Milland and William Holden, Paramount Pictures, 28" x 22". $150-$200

Ladies Courageous, 1944 (World War II)
Loretta Young and Geraldine Fitzgerald, Universal, 14" x 36". $75-$100

Lifeboat, 1944 (World War II)
Tallulah Bankhead and John Hodiak, 20th Century Fox, 27" x 41". $300-$400

The Longest Day, 1962 (World War II)
John Wayne and Henry Fonda, 20th Century Fox, 27" x 41". $200-$300

The Lost Squadron, 1932 (World War I)
Richard Dix, RKO-Radio Pictures, 27" x 41". $80-$95

Memphis Belle, 1944 (World War II)
8th Air Force, 27" x 41". $600-$700

Midway, 1955 (World War II)
Charlton Heston and Henry Fonda, 27" x 41". $300-$400

Objective Burma, 1944 (World War II)
Errol Flynn, William Prince, and James Brown, U.S. War Department, 27" x 41".
$250-$350

Okinawa, 1952 (World War II)
Pat O'Brien and Cameron Mitchell, Columbia Pictures, 27" x 41". $150–$250

One of Our Aircraft Is Missing, 1941 (World War II)
Godfrey Tearle and Eric Portman, British, 28" x 22". $150–$200

Over the Top, 1918 (World War I)
Arthur Guy Empey, Vitagraph Productions, 27" x 41". $300–$400

Parachute Battalion, 1941 (World War II)
Robert Preston and Edmond O'Brien, 27" x 41". $100–$125

Passage to Marseilles, 1944 (World War II)
Humphrey Bogart and Peter Lorre, U.S. War Department, 27" x 41". $400–$600

Paths of Glory, 1957 (World War I)
Kirk Douglas, United Artists, 27" x 41". $100–$125

Patton, 1969 (World War II)
George C. Scott and Karl Malden, 20th Century Fox, 27" x 41". $400–$500

**Pershings's Crusaders, Auspices of the United States Government,
the First Official American War Picture Taken by U.S. Signal Corps and Navy
Photographers, 1918 (World War I)**
Official U.S. war film, Committee on Public Information, 27" x 41". $600–$800

So Proudly We Hail, 1943 (World War II), Claudette Colbert and Paulette Goddard, Paramount Pictures, 27" x 41", $600–$800

The Pride of New York: A Stirring Patriotic Drama, 1917 (World War I)
William Fox and George Nash, Fox Film Corporation, 27" x 41". $125–$150

The Purple Heart, 1944 (World War II)
Dana Andrews and Richard Conte, 20th Century Fox, 27" x 41". $150–$200

The Red Baron, 1971 (World War I)
John Phillip Law, United Artists, 27" x 41". $50–$75

Remember Pearl Harbor, 1942 (World War II)
Donald M. Barry and Alan Curtis, Republic Pictures, 27" x 41". $600–$800

Rosie the Riveter, **1944 (World War II)**
Jane Frazee and Frank Albertson, Republic Pictures, 27" x 41". $300-$400

Sahara, **1945 (World War II)**
Humphrey Bogart and Lloyd Bridges, Columbia, 27" x 41". $600-$800

Sands of Iwo Jima, **1949 (World War II)**
John Wayne and John Agar, Republic Pictures, 27" x 41". $700-$900

Sergeant York, **1941 (World War I)**
Gary Cooper and Walter Brennan, U.S. War Department, 27" x 41". $400-$600

Ships and Wings, **1941 (World War II)**
John Clements and Leslie Banks, British, 27" x 41". $100-$150

Stalag 17, **1953 (World War II)**
William Holden and Otto Preminger, Paramount Pictures, 27" x 41". $500-$600

Stand By for Action, **1943 (World War II)**
Robert Taylor and Brian Donlevy, MGM, 14" x 22". $250-$350

The Story of GI Joe, **1945 (World War II)**
Burgess Meredith and Robert Mitchum, United Artists, 27" x 41". $350-$400

Thirty Seconds Over Tokyo, 1944 (World War II), Spencer Tracy, Van Johnson, and Robert Walker, MGM, 27 " x 41 ", $650-$750

They Died with Their Boots On, **1941 (World War II)**
Errol Flynn and Olivia de Havilland, U.S. War Department, 27" x 41". $350-$450

They Were Expendable, **1945 (World War II)**
Robert Montgomery and John Wayne, MGM, 27" x 41". $300-$400

Thunderbirds, **1942 (World War II)**
Preston Foster and Gene Tierney, 20th Century Fox, 14" x 36". $75-$100

To Hell and Back, **1955 (World War II)**
Audie Murphy and Marshall Thompson, United International, 27" x 41". $200-$300

To the Shores of Tripoli, **1942 (World War II)**
John Payne and Randolph Scott, 20th Century Fox, 28" x 22". $200-$300

Wake Island, 1942, Brian Donlevy, Macdonald Carey, and Robert Preston, Paramount Pictures, 27" x 41", $650-$750

Winged Victory, 1944, Clara Bow, 20th Century Fox, 27" x 41", $100-$125

Tunisian Victory, **1944 (World War II)**
The invasion and liberation of North Africa, documentary, 27" x 41". $300-$400

Twelve O'Clock High, **1949 (World War II)**
Gregory Peck, 20th Century Fox, 27" x 41". $600-$800

United We Stand, **1942 (World War II)**
Documentary, 20th Century Fox, 27" x 41". $75-$100

Wings: An Epic of the Air, **1927**
Paramount Pictures, 27" x 41". $75-$100

With the Marines at Tarawa, **1944**
U.S. Marine documentary, Universal, 27" x 41". $200-$400

Yank in the RAF, **1942**
Tyrone Power and Betty Grable, 20th Century Fox, 27" x 41". $900-$1000

Political Items

*P*olitical memorabilia has always stirred the interest of the collector because of links to past campaigns and political issues, but the collecting of political patriotic items has evoked an even deeper passion due to the association with the American flag, the eagle, the Statue of Liberty, World Wars I and II, and of course, Uncle Sam. The William Henry Harrison campaign of 1840 was the first political campaign where souvenirs (such as tokens, banners, neckties, and beanies) were given away to a candidate's supporters. Beginning with the 19th century, badges and pinback buttons displaying photographs of the candidates became very popular among the supporters of the candidate. Today the political button is one of the most sought-after political items, followed by banners, flags, and scarves.

With political patriotic collectibles, red, white, and blue material or colors are more desirable than black or white colors. While items that contain or depict the American flag or bald eagle are sought after more than other items, items such as black mourning ribbons or badges issued after the death of President Abraham Lincoln and worn at his funeral are highly desirable and very expensive.

Banner. Abraham Lincoln and Andrew Johnson Presidential Election, 1864
Grand national banner for the 1864 presidential election, Currier and Ives print.
$10,000

Zachary Taylor presidential campaign bandana, 1848, 24" x 24", $7,000. Photo from the collection of Howard Hazelcorn.

Bumper Ornament. "Drive Ahead with Roosevelt," 1936
Uncle Sam looking at Franklin D. Roosevelt with hands on Roosevelt's shoulder. Die-cut molded composition with gold, red, white, and dark blue paint, 8" x 11-1/4". Manufactured by ARPO, copyright 1936 by Nationwide Distributors, New York. $150–$175

Buttons

★ **Franklin D. Roosevelt, 1932–1936**
Black and white photograph with rim design on red, white, and blue. $35–$40

★ **Franklin D. Roosevelt Campaign, 1940**
Uncle Sam pointing his thumb down saying "No Third Term" (Franklin D. Roosevelt's campaign against Wendell Willkie), 3/4". $35–$45

★ **Franklin D. Roosevelt Inaugural Souvenir, January 2, 1941**
Black and white 1-1/4" button with 1-3/4" x 3-1/4" red, white, and blue ribbon reading "Inauguration, Franklin D. Roosevelt, Our First Third Term President/ January 2, 1941/Washington, D.C." $50–$60

★ **Harry S. Truman Inauguration, 1948**
Red, white, blue, 3-1/2" diameter, photograph in black and white center. $90–$100

Calendar. "Ship of State," 1916
Uncle Sam and Woodrow Wilson, "Straight Ahead, I'm Back of You," 15" x 20".
$15–$20

Clock. Pot Metal Clock, "United" and "Our Uncle Sam," 1944
Clock face marked "United" with eagle and star (which both light up) above it, base marked "Our Uncle Sam," 11-1/2" x 13" x 3-1/4". $400–$500
This clock commemorated Franklin D. Roosevelt's involvement in the North Atlantic Treaty Organization.

Envelopes. Civil War Patriotic Envelopes, 1861–1865 (three items)
Red, white, and blue patriotic envelopes: (1) envelope with hand-colored depiction of three men holding a "Union Forever" sign, (2) envelope with patriotic eagle and

William Henry Harrison presidential campaign flag, 1840, $27,000. Photo from the collection of Howard Hazelcorn.

Abraham Lincoln campaign flag, 1860, $7500-$8500. Notice misspelling of Lincoln's first name as "Abram." Photo from the collection of Howard Hazelcorn.

flowing American flag with a four-line verse about traitors, and (3) bright yellow envelope with design of American flag and cannon in red and blue with slogan "If Any Man Attempts to Haul Down the American Flag, Shoot Him on the Spot" (Gen. Dix. Exc.) $40 (all three)

Flags

★ **Florida Flag, 1860**

During the 1860 Republican Convention in Chicago, each state represented had to have a flag with its state's name. $900-$1000

Convention where Abraham Lincoln was nominated to run for the presidency.

★ **Abraham Lincoln Presidential Campaign Flag , 1860**

American flag reading "For President Abram Lincoln, For Vice President Hannibal Hamlin." $7500-$8500

(Note misspelling of Lincoln's first name as "Abram.")

★ **Wide Awake Organization, 1860**

Flag has blue top with picture of an eye reading "Wide Awake" with bottom showing a red, white, and red stripe, reading "Lincoln-Hamlin" on white stripe. $35,000

Flag was used by a pro-Lincoln organization to elect Lincoln to the presidency in 1860. Also used in a torchlight parade.

★ **Confederate Battle Flag, 1863**

Words on flag read "Taken from Rebels at Winchester." Hand-stitched with nine stars in circle (should be 10, one missing) and one star in middle. $22,000

William McKinley and Garret Hobart silk campaign flag, 1896, $16,000-$17,000. Photo from the collection of Howard Hazelcorn.

Jugate. William McKinley and Teddy Roosevelt, 1900

Black and white photographs of McKinley and Theodore Roosevelt, red, white, and blue accent bow, backpaper reads "National Equipment Co., Whitehead and Hoag." $20-$25

Lapel Stud. William McKinley, 1896

Black and white photograph in center, dark blue and bright red stars on cream rim. $20-$25

Medalet. Abraham Lincoln, 1860–1864

One side with spread-wing eagle and slogan "Success to Republican Principles," other side embossed "Millions for Freedom, Not One Cent for Slavery." $100-$125

Mourning Badge. Abraham Lincoln, 1865

Rosette-type black badge with photograph of Lincoln in center, with black ribbons. $700-$750

This badge was worn immediately after Lincoln's death and at the funeral.

Abraham Lincoln national inauguration ball invitation, 1860, with photograph of Abraham Lincoln and Andrew Johnson celebrating Lincoln's victory for president, $1700-$2000. Photo from the collection of Howard Hazelcorn.

Abraham Lincoln mourning ribbon, 1865, worn for two months after Lincoln's death, $275-$300; Abraham Lincoln and Andrew Johnson Union election ticket, 1864, $300-$375. Photo from the collection of Howard Hazelcorn.

Newspaper Supplement. Woodrow Wilson World War I Patriotic Newspaper Supplement, 1918

December 22, 1917, issue of *The Patriot* (Harrisburg, Pennsylvania, newspaper), calendar page, 10-$^3/_4$" x 13-$^3/_4$" silver accent wood frame with black accent trim. Photograph of Wilson above center set in art design of Allied flags. Bottom portion is monthly calendar for 1918 with doughboy on left and Navy man on right, both holding rifles. $10-$20

Pinback Buttons

★ **William Jennings Bryan, 1896**
   Picture of Bryan, red, white, and blue, 1-$^1/_4$". $30-$35

★ **William McKinley, 1896**
   The Syracuse Post, picture of McKinley, red, white, and blue, $^3/_4$" stud. $50-$55
   This stud is one of the earliest items of a presidential campaign and is a fantastic presidential collectible as well as a great journalistic collectible.

★ **William McKinley, 1896**
   Black and white photograph, $^7/_8$" diameter, gold trim, diamond design flanked by red, white, and blue stars and stripes motif, bright gold outer motif. $30-$35

★ **Henry R. Wolcott, 1898**
   "Colorado Statehood, For Governor Henry R. Wolcott," black and white photograph with red, white, and blue flag. $18-$20

★ **William McKinley and Theodore Roosevelt, 1900**
   Red, white, and blue ribbons, 1-$^1/_4$". $55-$60

★ **Theodore Roosevelt, 1904**
   "The Spirit Of The Republic, Success, President Of All The People," Uncle Sam standing at a gate to the White House with signs reading "Prejudice," "Lawlessness," and "Injustice," giving Roosevelt the sign reading "Prejudice. $1200-$1500

★ **Theodore Roosevelt, 1904**
   Roosevelt having lunch with black educator Booker T. Washington, an event that scandalized the South. Rare. $75-$100

★ **Woodrow Wilson, 1912-1916**
   Red, white, and blue, blue name, 1-$^7/_8$". $20-$25

★ **Charles Evan Hughes, 1916**
   Hughes campaign, red, white, and blue, $^5/_8$". $10-$12

★ **Charles Evan Hughes, 1916**
   The Women's Committee of the Charles Evans Hughes Alliance, in red, white, and blue shield. Scarce. $45-$50

★ "Votes For Women, Patriotism" 1918

Button is yellow with blue border and eagle with red, white, and blue stars and stripes in center. $35-$45

Early suffragette button honoring women's contributions during World War I.

★ Calvin Coolidge and Charles Dawes, 1924

Red, white, and blue, $7/8$". $5-$7

★ Al Smith, 1928

"Smith for President," red, white, and blue, $7/8$". $16-$18

★ Herbert Hoover, 1928

Red, white, and blue stars and stripes, $7/8$". $20-$22

★ Franklin D. Roosevelt, 1932

"The Union of Democratic Clubs, Roosevelt, Deputy," red, white, and blue, $1\text{-}1/4$".
$10-$12

★ Alf Landon, 1936

"Democrat for Landon," red, white, and blue, $7/8$". $15-$17

★ Wendell Willkie, 1940

"I Will Vote [picture of American flag] Willkie," red, white, and blue, $3/4$".
$30-$35

★ Wendell Willkie, 1940

Red, white, and blue, $1\text{-}1/4$". $13-$15

★ Franklin D. Roosevelt, 1940

"No Third Term," red, white, and blue, $7/8$". $25-$30

One of the biggest issues in the 1940 presidential campaign was whether Franklin D. Roosevelt should be allowed to serve a third term as president.

★ Uncle Sam, 1942

"Let's Pull Together," lever on left side activates Uncle Sam hanging Hitler.
$100-$125

★ Thomas Dewey, 1944–1948

"Vote Dewey for President," photograph of Dewey, red, white, and blue, $3\text{-}1/2$".
$8-$10

Made by Philadelphia Badge Company.

★ Thomas Dewey, 1948

"Dewey, I'm on the Team, Warren," red, white, and blue, $2\text{-}1/8$". $14-$16

★ Harry S. Truman, 1948

"4-H Club, Help Hustle Harry Home," red, white, and blue, $7/8$". $18-$20

★ Dwight D. Eisenhower, 1950

Picture of Eisenhower with Chinese language, red, white, and blue, $1\text{-}1/4$". $20-$25

★ **Dwight D. Eisenhower and Richard M. Nixon, 1952**
"Ike [photograph of Eisenhower and Nixon] Dick," red, white, and blue 3-^{1}/$_2$".
$24-$26

★ **Dwight D. Eisenhower, 1952-1956**
"For the Love of IKE, Vote Republican," picture of Eisenhower, red, white,
and blue, ^{7}/$_8$". $7-$9

★ **Adlai Stevenson, 1952-1956**
"All the Way with ADLAI," red, white, and blue, 3". $38-$40

★ **John F. Kennedy, 1960**
"Our Next President," photograph of Kennedy with a patriotic flag design, red,
white, and blue, 1-^{3}/$_4$". Rare. $495-$510

★ **John F. Kennedy, 1960**
"Kennedy [picture of Kennedy] COPE (Council on Political Education)," red,
white, and blue. $7-$9

★ **Richard M. Nixon, 1960**
"Vote for President, Richard M. Nixon," red, white, and blue, 3-^{1}/$_2$". $20-$22

★ **Richard M. Nixon, 1960**
"Nixon, Lodge," border of pin is red, eagle in back of photographs is blue, red,
and white, next to blue ribbons, rectangular, 2-^{3}/$_4$". $15-$17
Made by Fargo Rubber Stamp Works.

Postcards

★ **"My Choice, Taft For President", 1908**
Photograph of William Taft surrounded by American flag, eagle, and dove of
peace. $25-$35

★ **"Uncle Sam Wood-Row Wilson To The White House," 1912**
Uncle Sam in rowboat named "Progressive" with Woodrow Wilson rowing to
the White House, Theodore Roosevelt and William Howard Taft swimming
behind rowboat. $35-$45

★ **"Presidential Elections Of The U.S.A.," 1912**
Satiric French hand-drawn cartoon of Theodore Roosevelt and William
Howard Taft with American flag, 1912 presidential campaign. $300-$325

Portrait. William McKinley, 1900

Brass rim holds color portrait of McKinley, brass loop at top has red, white, and
blue fabric tied to small loop, 3-^{3}/$_4$" diameter. Scarce. $90-$100

Posters

★ "The Issue, 1900, Liberty, Justice, Humanity, No Crown Of Thorns, W. J. Bryan, No Cross Of Gold, Equal Rights To All, Special Privileges to None," 1900
Photograph of William Jennings Bryan with American flags on each side of photograph, with Liberty Bells in background reading "1776 Liberty" and "1900 No Imperialism." $200-$300
Poster used in Bryan's second unsuccessful attempt to beat William McKinley.

Major General George B. McClellan presidential campaign poster, 1864, showing McClellan riding horse with other soldiers, used in presidential campaign against Abraham Lincoln (Lincoln won), $2500. Photo from the collection of Howard Hazelcorn.

★ Abraham Lincoln, World War I "Liberty Bonds," 1916
Portrait of Lincoln above an excerpt from his Gettysburg Address, 20" x 30". $25-$30

★ "I Think We've Got Another Washington And Wilson Is His Name," 1917
Uncle Sam standing with red-striped shield in background and arms outstretched over photographs of George Washington and Woodrow Wilson, 20" x 16". $175-$200

★ "Making The World Safe For Democracy" and "Carrying The World To Victory," 1918
Uncle Sam standing with the world on his shoulders, eagle on top of the world, with U.S. and Allied flags on both sides of the world, photographs of President Woodrow Wilson and General John Pershing on either side of the world, 19-1/2" x 15-1/2". $275-$300

★ "Roosevelt For President," 1932-1936
Photograph of Franklin D. Roosevelt in circle of red, white stars, and blue, with red strip on border of poster and white stars with blue background in bottom left- and right-hand corners. Rare. $300-$400

★ Franklin D. Roosevelt
Red, white, and blue, bluestone photograph of Franklin D. Roosevelt and several Missouri Democrats, including Harry S. Truman for United States Senator, 11" x 14". $70-$80

Ribbons

★ **George Washington, 1832**
Issued for centennial of his birth. Oval portrait surrounded by flags and military equipment with rays above, reads "Centennial Celebration February 22, 1832," 1-³/4" x 7". $90-$110

★ **Abraham Lincoln "President Elect" Philadelphia Reception**
Dark blue silk ribbon with bright gold printing that reads "City Of Philadelphia" and "Reception Of Hon. Abraham Lincoln, President Elect Of The U.S., February 21, 1861," 2-³/4" x 8". Rare. $1300-$1400

★ **William McKinley, 1896**
"Our Standard," black and white, cream ground, brass eagle and flags bar pin hanger at top, 2-¹/2" x 7". $90-$100

★ **Woodrow Wilson Campaign, 1912–1916**
Campaign ribbon, red, white, and blue, "Democratic" ticket above and below crossed flags, 3" x 6". $35-$40

★ **Harry S. Truman Inauguration, 1948**
Ribbon badge, Democratic National Convention, Philadelphia, Pennsylvania, 1-¹/4" x 5-¹/2", brass and enamel, raised image of "Birthplace of Old Glory" with furling flags on either side, 1-¹/4" brass medal with raised image of William Penn, Liberty Bell, and Independence Hall. $50-$55

"President Lincoln's Grand March," 1864, sheet music, $350-$450. Photo from the collection of Howard Hazelcorn.

Ribbon Badge. "We Want Roosevelt"
Brass and fabric ribbon, red, white, and blue fabric, gold type, brass framed bar pin at top with blank cardboard insert for name, 1-³/4" x 5". $50-$60

Sheet Music. "President Lincoln's Grand March," 1864
"Respectfully Dedicated to THE UNION ARMY," by F. B. Helmsmuller. $350-$450

Sheet Music. Franklin D. Roosevelt, 1938
"On With Roosevelt," red, white, and blue, by Louise Graeser. $10-$15

Grover Cleveland versus Benjamin Harrison presidential campaign tie, 1888, chocolate brown tie sewn to maintain a permanent full Windsor, with the phrase "1888 Campaign" inside the neck loop, $100-$200

Sticker. "We Will Win, Forward Together With United Strength," 1942

President Franklin D. Roosevelt in middle of "V" symbol. $20-$25

Postcards

*I*f it were possible to have all the postcards that have ever been printed since the 1860s gathered up and bound into one large book, our country would have one of the best scrapbooks ever assembled. Since the first postcard was introduced in 1869, postcards have recorded our history, wars, social and political events (both good and disappointing), national parks, oceans, rivers, and towns small and large. Actually, the first postcard that was issued in 1869 was by the Austrian Postal Authority and then in 1870 by the North German Confederation. In 1870 the British and French began to print their own cards, which quickly won the approval of the local citizens. The first government postcard was issued on May 13, 1873. The best example of a picture postcard in America was for the Industrial Exposition in Chicago in 1873. The postcard soon became the best and most inexpensive form of communication, long before the television, computers, radios, and phones and became a mainstay in many political campaigns. On May 19, 1898, printers and publishers in the United States were allowed to finally produce their own postcards, with the actual production date being July 1, 1898. This also began the era of private cards, souvenir and patriotic cards, and greeting cards of every type imaginable.

As the United States entered a series of wars beginning with Spanish-American War and exploding into World War I and World War II, postcards became a quick communication device to show off our patriotism and support our fighting men and women around the world.

Boeing B-17 Flying Fortress, Color Photo, Linen, 1941–1945
Art Colortone. $5-$10

"Brothers Still, 'Tis God's Will," 1907
Uncle Sam shaking hands with an Irish lad. $25-$35

"The Birth Of Our Flag," 1910, picture of four ladies sewing American flag and Betsy Ross House, Philadelphia, Pennsylvania, 5-½" x 3-½', $7-$10

Civil War UCV Flags VA, 1907
"1861–1865. Our battle-flags! By the bravest of the brave were borne, As Symbols of the patriot trust. Souvenir. Confederate Reunion. Richmond, Virginia, 1907." $300-$325

"Defend Your Country"
Large blue "V" with Uncle Sam in background, hat removed, rolling up sleeves, and fists clenched. $5-$10

"Defend Your Country 'V,'" 1941
Tichnor Bros., color, linen. $5-$10

"Dollars for Bonds Means Weapons to Win/Make Every Payday a Bond Day," 1941–1945
Graycraft Card Company, black and white photo. $5-$10

Flag Celebration, Patriotic New York "Centennial Celebration 1807–1907"
Cooperstown, New York, large U.S. flag in center. $20-$25

"The Glorious Fourth of July," 1910, $15-$20

"Fort Ferry, New York"
Crossed flags with eagle in center, embossed. $30-$35

"Fourth of July Greetings," 1890–1920
Young Uncle Sam holding U.S. flag with young lady, both dressed in red, white, and blue, Raphael Tuck & Sons. $60-$70

"4th of July," 1890–1920
Uncle Sam holding firecrackers that spell out "4th of July" and young boy holding U.S. flag, Raphael Tuck & Sons. $100-$110

"Gee! But I wish I was growed up," 1917
Little boy holding American flag in front of recruiting office with Uncle Sam blowing trumpet. $35-$45

"The Great Friend, American World War I Soldier"
World War I French-American relations, American soldier with U.S. flag in background, surrounded by French children. $25-$35

U.S. flag with George Washington in center of star, 1907, $100-$125

"The Great Seal of the State of Utah, 1896"
Eagle flag, published by Geo. F. Evans, Salt Lake City, Utah. $20-$25

"Hands Across the Sea," 1907
Uncle Sam holding his hand out to John Bull, who is saying, "Here's To You Uncle Sam May Your Shadow Never Grow Less," and Uncle Sam saying, "Same to You John." $20-$25

"Hurrah! For the Fourth of July Hurrah!" 1890–1920
Uncle Sam kissing the hand of Miss Liberty, stone lithograph and embossed "Post Card" in 14 languages on the back. $65-$75

"Liberty Day, Saturday, October 12th 1918, Buy Liberty Bonds Today For Liberty Today Tomorrow And Forever," 1918, $100

"I'm All Out for Victory," 1942 (World War II)
$5-$10

"I'm Your Air Raid Warden Lady; Put Out Your Lights and Cooperate," 1941–1945
Asheville Post Card Company, linen. $5-$10

"Independence Day July the Fourth, Novelty Firecracker," 1906
Foldout opens to a firecracker, Leighton, Pennsylvania. $65-$75

"In God We Trust To Save America," 1941
Harry Reiter, New York, eagle on front with "E Pluribus Unum" flags, flags of other countries on right side, 3-1/2" x 5". $50-$60

"Keep 'Em Flying" (World War II)
Large red "V" with dive bombers and large eagle. $5-$10

"Keep 'Em Flying" (World War II)
U.S. flag with fighter bomber. $5-$10

Lady Liberty Postcards, 1910
Postcards (made in Germany) depict Lady Liberty posing in front of American flag, 3-1/2" x 5-1/2". $10-$20 (each)
★ "Honor The Brave," 1861-1865
★ "With our beauty no flag can compare. All nations honor our banner so fair."
★ "Unfurl the glorious banner, let it wave upon the breeze. The emblem of our country's pride on land and on the seas."
★ "Unfurl on high the stars and stripes and let all nations see. How much we love old glory, the emblem of the free
★ "Nobly the flag flutters o'er us today. Emblem of peace, pledge of liberty's sway."
★ "The stars and stripes, loved and honored by all, Shall float on forever where freedom may call."

Navy Flag (Real Photo) (World War I)
Navy personnel holding U.S. flag during parade. $30-$35

"No Room For Rumors" (World War II)
Uncle Sam pointing finger, published by Seagram Distillers Corp., New York City. $45-$55

"Loose Lips Might Sink Ships," World War II, $45

"No Room for Rumors," World War II, $45-$55

"Old Glory," 1917, American flag, $10-$15

"Over The Top for Victory," 1941 (World War II)
$5-$10

Patriotic Postcards, 1917–1918
Each card depicts different arrangements of the American flag with various slogans, 3-^{1}/$_2$" x 5-^{1}/$_5$".
$10-$15 (each)

★ "Our Flag, Your Flag, Victorious in a Thousand Battles, Here's to Another Victory"
★ "Stars and Stripes Fearlessly Floating for Humanity & Democracy"
★ "Our Flag, Champion of the Oppressed, Liberty Forever"
★ "Here's to Our Glorious Flag, Untarnished, Unsullied, Unbeaten"
★ "FLAG of the Free, FIGHT TO KEEP IT FREE"
★ "STAND BY Your Colors & YOUR COLORS WILL STAND BY YOU"

President Wilson flag, 1917, $40-$45

"Pledge of Allegiance" (World War II)
U.S. flag surrounded by Army, Navy, Marines, and Navy fighter pilot. $5-$10

"Remember Pearl Harbor, One Hour of Total War, One American's Contribution to Help End This Terrible Mess, One Hour Sooner" (World War II)
"V" symbol with airplanes, tank, Navy, soldier, battleship, sculpture of Statue of Liberty in background. $75-$85

"Remember Pearl Harbor, We'll Get 'em in the End," 1941–1945
E. C. Kropp Company, 18 other postcards in foldout pack, color, linen. $25-$30

"Sammy," 1905
Portion of a song at top of card with Uncle Sam tipping his hat to Miss Canada, shield with stars and stripes in background. $40-$50

"So We'll Meet Again/Buy More War Bonds," 1941–1945
U.S. Treasury Department, color. $5-$10

"Ring It Again, Buy U.S. Gov't Bonds, Third Liberty Loan," 1917, $100

"Strive for Victory," 1941 (World War II)
$5–$10

Surrender of Burgoyne, Saratoga (October 17, 1777), 1917
General Burgoyne in the act of offering his sword to General Gates. $7–$12

Surrender of Cornwallis, U.S. Capitol, 1917
Officers of the British Army, passing the American and French guards and entering between the two lines of victors. $7–$12

Thanksgiving, 1910
Uncle Sam standing next to two turkeys, postmark November 1910. $25–$30

"That's Uncle Sam and maybe I'm not proud of him," July 2, 1917
Little boy pointing to picture of Uncle Sam. $20–$25

"Uncle Sam Says: The Peace of a Nation is its Greatest Asset"
Uncle Sam standing and holding cane with head of eagle. $25–$30

"A Square Deal For Every Man," 1908, President Theodore Roosevelt with American flag, $45–$50

"Uncle Sam Suffragee"
Uncle Sam dressed in red, white, and blue dress of stars and stripes. $45–$55

United States Army "V" (World War II)
Distributed free at Army bases during World War II. $5–$10

"United We Stand" (World War II)
U.S. flag with large "V" in middle. $25–$35

"Victory" (World War II)
U.S. flag in background. $4–$8

"Victory Is Our Goal," 1941 (World War II)
Tichnor Bros. $5–$10

Taft for president campaign, 1908, $65-$75

"We'll Get 'em in the End," 1941–1945
E. C. Kropp Company, color, linen.
$10-$15

"When this gentleman takes off his coat, he means business," 1890–1920
Illustrated by Postal Card & No. Company, New York, Uncle Sam with mean look rolling up his sleeves. $20-$25

"William H. Taft for President"
Picture of Taft with American flag in background. $10-$15

"You can Help your Uncle Sam
Win the War," 1917, patriotic
design from a poster promoting
War Savings Stamps, $100-$125

"WIN we WILL" (World War II)
U.S. flag in background. $5-$10

Sheet Music

ext to postcards, sheet music provides one of the most interesting, colorful, and historical glimpses into the patriotism of America. Sheet music has been in existence for more than 200 years, providing the music collector interested in patriotic themes an endless array of subjects. For the art collector, the lithography, engraving, and early examples of printmaking afford a unique and intriguing collection of one-of-a-kind art treasures. The majority of music collectors specialize in specific categories, such as sports, Prohibition, Broadway plays, political issues, and of course, patriotism. Patriotism and sheet music quickly became a mainstay of American music.

With the entry of the United States into World War I, patriotic sheet music quickly became one of the most popular forms of supporting our troops and keeping the spirits of America high. One of the most popular of these tunes was "Over There" by George M. Cohan in 1917, which a year later became a Norman Rockwell cover on *Life* magazine. A little more than 20 years later, this unique form of patriotism once again took on a new life, with the bombing of Pearl Harbor and the entry of the United States into World War II. Once again, America's fighting men and women needed support and an uplifting of spirits, and a whole new set of tunes made America and the world take notice.

Sheet music is a fun and inexpensive form of collecting and offers something for everyone.

"After The Battle Is Over, Then You Can Come Back to Me," 1918
L. Wolfe Gilbert and Anatol Friedland. $15-$20

"After The War is Over Will There Be Any 'Home Sweet Home,'" 1917
E. J. Pourmon and Joseph Woodruff. $15-$20

"The Air Corps Song," 1939–1942
Capt. Crawford and Carl Fisher. $15-$20

"America Here's My Boy," 1917
Andrew B. Sterling and Arthur Lange. $20-$25

"America, He's For You," 1918
Andrew B. Sterling, Joe Morris Music Company. Shows Uncle Sam with photographs of young boys and soldiers. $20-$25

"A-M-E-R-I-C-A Means I Love You My Yankee Land," 1917
Jack Frost. $10-$15

"American First," 1916
James Brockman. Shows picture of Uncle Sam and Miss Liberty. $25-$30

"America, Make The World Safe For Democracy," 1918
DeVivo and Levy. $15-$20

"American Victory Songs," 1942
Eckstein, Carl Fisher, Inc., New York. $10-$15

"Any Bonds Today?," 1941, Irving Berlin and Henry Morgenthau, Jr. (Secretary of the Treasury), $15-$20

"America United," 1921
Sam A. Perry, Belwind, Inc. Shows Uncle Sam holding map of United States. $30-$35

"Anchors Aweigh," 1943
Capt. Miles and Zimmermann, Robbins Music Corp. $15-$20

"Are You A True American?," 1917
Margaret Jeffries Timmons, Mishawaka, Indiana. Shows Uncle Sam standing in front of Statue of Liberty. $20-$25

"The Badge of Honor," 1918
M. L. Bean. Shows Uncle Sam holding badge that reads "World Peace." $15-$20

"The Ballad Of The Green Berets," 1966
Barry Sadler and Robin Moore. $5-$10

"Batter Up, Uncle Sam Is At The Plate," 1918
Tighe. $20-$25

"Battle Hymn," 1908
Julia Ward Howe and Charles Marshall. $10-$15

"The Caissons Go Rolling Along,"
1936, $35-45

"Battle Of The Nations," 1915
E. T. Paull Music Company. $30-$35

"The Birth Of A Nation," 1915
Allen. $15-$20

"The Birth Of Our Flag," 1898
Walter V. Ullner. $20-$25

"Bring Out The Flag Boys," 1876
John Ford. $20-$25

"Bugle Call Rag," 1916
J. Hubert Blake and Carey Morgan. $20-$25

"The Call Of The Flag," 1917
L.D. W. and H. Aide. $10-$15

"Cheer Up, Uncle Sam!" 1943
Mark Minkus and Henry Kane, Patriotic Music Pub., New York. $30-$35

"Comin' In On a Wing and a Prayer," 1943
Harold Admanson and Jimmy McHugh, Robbins Music Corp. $15-$20

"Commodore Dewey's Victory March," 1898
George Maywood. Dedicated to the American heroes of the Battle of Manila.
$35-$40

"The Dear Old Stars and Stripes," 1905
Reynolds. $15-$20

"Dear Old Uncle Sam," 1918
Henry I. Marshall. $15-$20

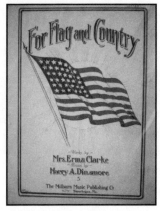

"For Flag and Country," 1915,
$35-$45

"Father of the Land We Love," 1931
George M. Cohan, Sol Bloom. George Washington on front, artist: James Montgomery Flagg. $10-$12

"The Finest Flag That Flies," 1916
Hughes and Richardson. $15-$20

"For Old Glory, Uncle Sam, We Are Preparing," 1917
Irving. $20-$25

"For The Honor Of The Flag," 1918
Raymond Hubbell. $15-$20

"For You And The Grand Old Flag," 1910
Coleman. $15-$20

"For Your Boy and My Boy," 1918
Gus Kahn and Egbert Van Alstyne. $15-$20

"For Your Country And My Country," 1917
Irving Berlin. Shows Uncle Sam playing drum with eagle on shoulder. $25-$35

"For the Red, White, and Blue,"
1898, $75-$100

"Give A Bonus To Our Men, In Honor of U.S. Veterans, Buck Privates Society," 1917
Russ Collier and Ben Seigel, Collier & Seigel Publishing Company. Shows Uncle Sam giving bonus checks to veterans. $20-$25

"God Bless America," 1939
Irving Berlin. $10-$15

"The Good Old U.S.A. March Song," 1917
Jack Drislane and Theodore Morse, F. D. Haviland Publishing Company. Shows Uncle Sam holding the hand of Miss Liberty. $50-$60

"Hats Off To the Red White and Blue," 1918
Ralph F. Beegan. $15-$20

"Here's To Your Boy And My Boy," 1918
George Fairman. Shows woman with red, white, and blue dress. $10-$15

"He's 1-A in the Army," 1943
Redd Evans, Valiant Music Company. With blue and white cover. $5-$7

"He Wears A Pair Of Silver Wings," 1941
Eric Maschwitz and Michael Carr. $5-$10

"He's My Uncle," 1940,
Charles Newman and Lew Pollack,
Bregman, Vocco and Conn,
$20-$25

"How About A Cheer For The Navy," 1942
Irving Berlin. From the movie *This Is the Army*.
$20-$25

"I Am An American," 1940
Paul Cunningham and Leonard Whitcup. $5-$10

"I Think We've Got Another Washington and Wilson Is His Name," 1917
George Fairman, Kendis-Brockman Music Company. Shows Uncle Sam standing next to photographs of Washington and Wilson. $40-$50

"It's A Long, Long Way To Tipperary," 1912
Jack Judge and Harry Williams. $20-$30

"It's The Flag," 1918
Lottie Simmons. $15-$20

"Let Freedom Ring," 1940
Shelley and Mossman. $10-$15

"Let The Flag Fly," 1917
L. Wolfe Gilbert. $15-$20

"Liberty Bell, It's Time To Ring Again," 1917
Joe Goodwin and Halsey K. Mohr. $10-$15

"The Liberty Bell March," 1898
John Philip Sousa. $25-$30

"Liberty Statue Is Looking Right At You," 1918
Guy Emprey. $50-$60

"Make Uncle Sam Your Banker," 1942
Photo of children lining up to buy war stamps from Uncle Sam. $20-$25

"March of the Boy Scouts," 1935, $25-$35

"The Marine's Hymn," 1919
L. Z. Phillips. $20-$25

"Meaning Of U.S.A.," 1902
Raymond Browne. $10-$15

"Military Parade," 1905
Chapman. $10-$15

"Miss America"
J. Edmund Barnum. Shows woman with stars, red and white dress, large flowing flag. $15-$20

"Miss Liberty," 1897
Andrew B. Sterling and Harry Von Tilzer. $15-$20

"Miss Liberty," 1949
Irving Berlin. $10-$15

"My Country Has First Call," 1910
Mack Gordon. $10-$15

"My Country I Hear You Calling Me," 1916
Bernie Grossman and Dave Dreyer. $10-$15

"My Country 'Tis Of Thee," 1917
Jack Stern. $10-$15

"My Land, My Flag," 1918
Zoel J. Parenteau. $10-$15

"National Defense Military March," 1916
J. Bodewalt Lampe. $15-$20

"National Emblem March," 1911
E. E. Bagley. Shows waving flag on cover. $15-$20

"Neath The Stars and Stripes," 1943
R. S. Morrison. $5-$10

"The Old Flag Never Touched The Ground," 1901
J. W. Johnson, Bob Cole, and Rosamond Johnson. $25-$30

"Old Glory," 1942
Johnny Mercer and Harold Arlen. From the movie *Star Spangled Rhythm*. $10-$20

"Our Banner Of Glory," 1861, national hymn of the Civil War, $150

"Old Glory Goes Marching On," 1918
Paul R. Armstrong and F. Henri Klickmann. $15-$20

"Old Glory I Salute You," 1929
Vaughn DeLeath. $25-$30

"Only For Americans," 1949
Irving Berlin. From the musical *Miss Liberty*. $10-$15

"Our Country's In It Now! We've Got To Win It Now!" 1918
Guy Empey. $50-$60

"Our Flag," 1859
Clark. $25-$30

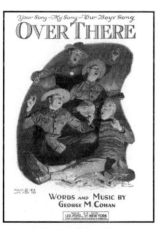

"Over There," 1917, George M. Cohan, with Norman Rockwell cover, $75-$85

"Our 'V' For Victory," 1942
Francis Wheeler. $10-$15

"Praise the Lord and Pass the Ammunition," 1942
Frank Loesser, Famous Music Company. $20-$25

"The Ragtime Soldier Man," 1912
Irving Berlin. $25-$35

"The Ragtime Volunteers Are Off To War," 1917
Ballard MacDonald. $15-$20

"Remember Pearl Harbor," 1941
Don Reid and Sammy Kaye, Republic Music Corp. $15-$20

"The Road to Victory," 1943
Frank Loesser, Pacific Music Sales. $10-$15

"Rosie The Riveter," 1942
Evans, Paramount Music, New York. $15-$20

"Salute The Flag," 1914
Victor Bartlett. $15-$20

"Salute To America," 1904
Harry J. Lincoln. $10-$15

"The Sammies Are Coming: The Song Hit of the Allied Countries," 1917
Walter S. Hunt and E. A. Powell, Hunt and Powell Publishing Company. Shows
Uncle Sam yelling across sea to British soldier. $30-$35

"Say A Prayer For The Boys Over There," 1943
Herb Magidson and Jimmy McHugh. $8-$10

"Shout Hurrah For America," 1914
Freeman. $15-$20

"Spirit Of America," 1917
J. S. Zamecnik. $15-$20

"Spirit Of Freedom," 1905
Abe Losch. $35-$40

"The Spirit Of The U.S.A.," 1908
Sprecht. $20-$25

"Stand By Uncle Sam," 1917
Sergeant Vernon T. Stevens, Charles Roat Music Company. $40-$45

"Stars and Stripes Are Calling," 1918
N. J. Kirk. $15-$20

"Stars and Stripes Forever March"
John Phillip Sousa, John Church Company. John Phillip Sousa portrait in upper
left-hand corner and Old Glory in center. $15-$20

"Stars & Stripes On Iwo Jima," 1945
Bob Wills and Cliff Johnson. $10-$15

"The Star-Spangled Banner," 1942
Francis Scott Key and John Stafford Smith. $10-$15

"The Statue Of Liberty Is Smiling," 1918
Jack Mahoney and Halsey K. Mohr. $20-$25

"The Stars and Stripes: Uncle Sam and You," 1917, $25-$35

"Story Of Old Glory, The Flag We Love," 1916
J. Will Callahan and Earnest R. Ball. $5-$7

"Thank God For America," 1918
Madalyn Phillips. $10-$15

"Thank You America," 1918
Walter Jurmann. $10-$15

"Thank Your Lucky Stars and Stripes," 1941
Johnny Burke and Jimmy Van Heusen. $10-$15

**"That's What The Red White and Blue Means,"
1918**
Robert Levenson and E. E. Bagley. $10-$15

"There's a Star Spangled Banner Waving Somewhere," 1942
Paul Roberts and Shelby Darnell, Bob Miller Inc. $10-$15

"This Is The Army," 1942
Irving Berlin, Army Emergency Relief. $15-$20

"To Our Army And Navy, U.S.A.," 1916
Kate Baldwin and Harry J. Lincoln, Harry J. Lincoln Music Company. Shows Uncle Sam marching with rifle. $35-$40

"Uncle Sam, Hold Your Flag Up High"
Pheiffer. $15-$20

"Uncle Sammy March Two-Step," 1904
Abe Holzmann, Leo Feist Publishing Company. Shows Uncle Sam standing by map of United States. $25-$30

"Under Any Old Flag At All," 1907
George M. Cohan. $15-$20

"Under One Flag," 1916
Jefford. $15-$20

"Under The American Eagle," 1901
Jacob Henry Ellis. $20-$25

"Under The Stars & Stripes," 1930
T. Roosevelt. $5-$10

"V for Victory is our Shield," 1942
Mark Minkus and Henry Kane, Patriotic Music Pub., New York. $10-$15

"Victory Polka," 1943
Samuel Cahn and Jule Styne. Red, white, and blue cover with stars and "V" symbol.
$8-$10

"Wake Up American," 1916
George Graff, Jr. and Jack Glogau, Leo Feist Publishing. This Is The Song That
Inspired All America. Shows Uncle Sam picking up pieces of destroyed ships.
$35-$45

"We Did It Before and We Can Do It Again," 1941
Cantor, Witmark & Sons. With Uncle Sam on cover. $10-$15

"We'll Carry The Star Spangled Banner Thru The Trenches," 1916
Daisy M. Erd, published by District Welfare Aide. Shows Uncle Sam holding
the flag. $25-$35

"We'll Fight For Uncle Sammy," 1918
Howard Reese and Keith Reese, Howard Reese Publishing Company. $15-$20

"We Must Be Vigilant," 1942
Edgar Leslie and Joseph Burke, Bregman, Vocco and Conn. From the movie *When
Johnny Comes Marching Home*. $10-$15

"We're Going Over," 1917
Andrew B. Sterling, Bernice Grossman, and Arthur Lange. $25-$30

"We're Going To Kick The Hell Out of Will-hell-em," 1917
Louis Matthew Long, McGarry-Long Music Publishing Company. Shows Uncle Sam kicking German leader Willhelem to the devil. $35-$45

"What Are You Going To Do To Help The Boys – Buy A Liberty Bond," 1918
Gus Kahn and Egbert Van Alstyne, Jerome H. Remick and Company. $25-$30

"What Kind Of An American Are You?" 1917
Lew Brown, Chas. McCarron, and Albert Von Tilzer, Broadway Music. Shows Uncle Sam pointing. $25-$30

"You'll Be There," 1915
J. Kiern Brennan and Ernest R. Ball, M. Witmark & Sons. Shows Uncle Sam pointing. $60-$70

"Young America, We're Strong For You," 1915
William J. McKenna. $15-$20

"You're A Grand Old Flag," 1906
George M. Cohan. $20-$25

Stamps

I think that everyone at some point in their lives has either held on to special or unique stamps or actually collected a series of stamps. Stamp collecting is one of those hobbies that is easy and inexpensive to start and offers one of the best and easiest lessons in American history. One of the most popular ways of collecting is to join a stamp club. Meetings are often held at schools, libraries, or community centers. All you need to do is ask your local postmaster or librarian for the locations of stamp clubs in your area.

Patriotism has long been a favorite subject for issues of all stamps, dating back to 1847 up to present-day issues. Beginning with the signers of the Declaration of Independence to presidents of the United States, stamps have covered an array of subjects, with flags, the Statue of Liberty, and World Wars I and II being among the most popular. As will be noted with the following selection of patriotic stamps, America has long shown its love, fascination, and history of patriotism through the eyes of the artists who design and define stamps that tell a story in a single picture.

Francis Scott Key 3¢, August 9, 1948, unused 15¢-20¢, used 15¢-20¢

Independence (Sesquicentennial Exposition) 2¢, May 10, 1926, unused $3-$4, used 50¢-$1

Description	Unused	Used
AMERICAN BICENTENNIAL ISSUE		
Spirit of 76 (three stamps) 13¢—1/1/76		
Drummer Boy	25¢-30¢	25¢-30¢
Old Drummer	25¢-30¢	25¢-30¢
Fife Player	25¢-30¢	25¢-30¢
The Surrender of Lord Cornwallis at Yorktown by John Trumbull 18¢—5/29/76		
Two American Officers	45¢-50¢	45¢-50¢
General Benjamin Lincoln	45¢-50¢	45¢-50¢
George Washington	45¢-50¢	45¢-50¢
John Trumbull, Col. David Cobb, General Friedrich von Steuben, Marquis de Lafayette, and Thomas Nelson	45¢-50¢	45¢-50¢
Alexander Hamilton, John Laurens, and Walter Stewart	45¢-50¢	45¢-50¢
Washington Crossing the Delaware 24¢—5/29/76		
Boatman	70¢-80¢	70¢-80¢
George Washington	70¢-80¢	70¢-80¢
Flagbearer	70¢-80¢	70¢-80¢
Men in Boat	70¢-80¢	70¢-80¢
Steersman and Men on Shore	70¢-80¢	70¢-80¢
Washington Reviewing His Ragged Army at Valley Forge 31¢—5/29/76		
Two Officers	85¢-95¢	85¢-95¢
George Washington	85¢-95¢	85¢-95¢
Officer and Brown Horse	85¢-95¢	85¢-95¢
White Horse and Officer	85¢-95¢	85¢-95¢
Three Soldiers	85¢-95¢	85¢-95¢
AMERICAN REVOLUTION		
Valley Forge 2¢—5/26/28	$1-$2	35¢-40¢
American Revolution Bicentennial 1776–1976 8¢—7/4/71	20¢-25¢	20¢-25¢
Armed Forces Reserve 3¢—5/21/55	15¢-20¢	15¢-20¢
Bald Eagle 10¢—12/01/11	$65-$75	$7-$8
Betsy Ross 3¢—1/02/52	15¢-20¢	15¢-20¢
CAPITOL DOME SERIES		
Head of Freedom $5—3/20/23	$150-$160	$14-$16
Statue of Freedom 3¢—4/20/50	15¢-20¢	15¢-20¢

Description	Unused	Used
DECLARATION OF INDEPENDENCE		
Declaration of Independence 24¢—1875	$6000-$7000	$700-$800
Declaration of Independence 13¢—7/4/76		
Delegates	25¢-30¢	15¢-20¢
Delegates and John Adams	25¢-20¢	15¢-20¢
Roger Sherman, Robert R. Livingston, Thomas Jefferson, Benjamin Franklin	25¢-30¢	15¢-20¢
John Hancock, Charles Thomson, George Read, John Dickinson, Edward Rutledge	25¢-30¢	15¢-20¢
DRAFTING OF THE CONSTITUTION—8/28/87		
The Bicentennial	55¢-65¢	20¢-25¢
We The People	55¢-65¢	20¢-25¢
Establish Justice	55¢-65¢	20¢-25¢
And Secure	55¢-65¢	20¢-25¢
Do Ordain	55¢-65¢	20¢-25¢
Abraham Lincoln Quotation 4¢—9/14/60	20¢-25¢	20¢-25¢
Battle of Bunker Hill 10¢—6/17/75	20¢-25¢	20¢-25¢
Battle of Lexington & Concord 10¢—4/19/75 "Birth Of Liberty"	20¢-25¢	20¢-25¢
Bill of Rights 25¢—9/25/89 U.S. flag, eagle with quill pen in mouth	45¢-50¢	20¢-25¢
Boston Tea Party 8¢—7/4/73	20¢-25¢	20¢-25¢
Eagle and Moon $9.35—1983	$20-$22	$13-$15
Eagle and Moon $10.75—4/29/85	$20-$21	$7-$8
Eagle and Moon $8.75—10/04/88	$13-$14	$8-$9
Francis Scott Key Quotation 4¢—9/14/60	20¢-25¢	20¢-25¢
George Washington 20¢—2/2/82 Flag in background	40¢-50¢	20¢-25¢
Girl Scout Jubilee (flag background) 4¢—7/24/62	15¢-20¢	15¢-20¢
Gold Star Mothers (single star) 3¢—9/21/48	15¢-20¢	15¢-20¢
Great Seal of the United States 16¢—8/30/34	55¢-60¢	50¢-55¢
Head of Liberty 16¢—3/31/78	30¢-35¢	15¢-20¢
Independence Hall 10¢—7/4/74	20¢-25¢	20¢-25¢
Peace Corps, Flags & Doves 8¢—2/11/72	20¢-25¢	20¢-25¢
Constitution and Signer's Hand Holding Quill Pen 22¢—9/17/87	45¢-50¢	20¢-25¢

Description	Unused	Used
FLAG SERIES		
49-Star Flag 4¢—7/4/59	15¢-20¢	15¢-20¢
50-Star Flag 4¢—7/4/60	15¢-20¢	15¢-20¢
50- and 13-Star Flags 10¢—12/8/73	15¢-20¢	15¢-20¢
Flag over White House 5¢—1/9/63	15¢-20¢	15¢-20¢
Flag over Capitol 13¢—3/11/77	20¢-25¢	20¢-25¢
Flag over Capitol 22¢—3/29/85	35¢-40¢	15¢-20¢
Flag over White House 6¢—1/24/68	15¢-20¢	15¢-20¢
Flag over White House 29¢—4/23/92	50¢-55¢	20¢-25¢
Flag over Independence Hall 13¢—11/15/75	20¢-25¢	15¢-20¢
Flag over Supreme Court 20¢—12/17/81	35¢-40¢	15¢-20¢
Register to Vote with Flag 5¢—8/1/64	15¢-20¢	15¢-20¢
United States Savings Bonds 5¢—10/26/66	15¢-20¢	15¢-20¢
We Appreciate Our Servicemen	15¢-20¢	15¢-20¢
Flag and Anthem 18¢—4/24/81		
"... For Amber Waves Of Grain"	25¢-30¢	15¢-20¢
"... From Sea To Shining Sea"	25¢-30¢	15¢-20¢
"... For Purple Mountain Majesties"	25¢-30¢	15¢-20¢
Flag with Fireworks 22¢—5/9/87	35¢-40¢	15¢-20¢
Flag with Clouds 25¢—5/6/88	45¢-50¢	20¢-25¢
Flag over Yosemite 25¢—5/20/88	45¢-50¢	20¢-25¢
Flag, Single Pane 25¢—5/18/90	50¢-55¢	25¢-30¢
Flag over Mt. Rushmore 29¢—3/29/91	50¢-55¢	20¢-25¢
Flag, Olympic Rings 29¢—4/21/91	50¢-55¢	20¢-25¢
Flags on Parade 29¢—5/30/91	45¢-50¢	15¢-20¢
Flag, I Pledge Allegiance 29¢—9/8/92	50¢-55¢	20¢-25¢

Flag 4¢, July 4, 1957,
unused 15¢-20¢, used 15¢-20¢

Eagle and Shield 10¢, 1875,
unused $1700-$1900,
used $130-$150

Eagle and Shield 13¢,
December 1, 1975,
unused 20¢-25¢,
used 15¢-20¢

Description	Unused	Used
HISTORICAL FLAG ISSUE 7/04/68		
Ft. Moultrie Flag (1776) 6¢	35¢-40¢	20¢-25¢
Ft. McHenry Flag (1795–1818) 6¢	25¢-30¢	20¢-25¢
Washington's Cruiser's Flag (1775)	20¢-25¢	20¢-25¢
Bennington Flag (1777)	20¢-25¢	20¢-25¢
Rhode Island Flag (1775)	20¢-25¢	20¢-25¢
First Stars and Stripes (1777)	20¢-25¢	20¢-25¢
Bunker Hill Flag (1775)	20¢-25¢	20¢-25¢
Grand Union Flag (1776)	20¢-25¢	20¢-25¢
Philadelphia Light Horse Flag (1775)	20¢-25¢	20¢-25¢
First Navy Jack (1775)	20¢-25¢	20¢-25¢
Liberty Bell 13¢—10/31/75	25¢-30¢	15¢-20¢
Liberty Bell (carmine) 2¢—1926	$1-$1.25	45¢-50¢
Korean War Veterans 22¢—7/26/85	35¢-40¢	15¢-20¢
Organized Labor, Proud and Free—9/1/80 Bald Eagle 15¢	30¢-35¢	30¢-35¢
Moon Landing $2.40—7/20/89 Astronauts holding American flag	$4-$4.50	$2-$2.50
Savings Bonds (eagle with flag background) 29¢—4/30/91	45¢-50¢	15¢-20¢
USA Circle of Stars 6¢—4/24/81	40¢-50¢	20¢-25¢
We Appreciate Our Servicemen United States Savings Bond 5¢—10/26/66	20¢-25¢	20¢-25¢
SHIELD AND EAGLE SERIES		
Eagle and Shield 25¢—11/10/89	50¢-55¢	20¢-25¢
Eagle Holding Shield, Olive Branch, and Arrows 6¢—5/14/38	45¢-50¢	15¢-20¢
Ultramarine and Carmine	$140-$150	
Vertical pair, imperf. horizontally	$325-$350	
Horizontal pair, imperf. vertically	$12,000-$13,000	
SHIELD, EAGLE, AND FLAGS SERIES		
Shield, Eagle, and Flags 30¢—1875	$6000-$7000	$500-$600
STATUE OF LIBERTY SERIES		
Statue of Liberty 15¢—11/11/22	$22-$25	15¢-20¢
Statue of Liberty 3¢—6/24/54	15¢-20¢	15¢-20¢
Statue of Liberty 8¢—4/9/54	20¢-25¢	15¢-20¢
Statue of Liberty 3¢—10/1/56	20¢-25¢	20¢-25¢
Statue of Liberty 11¢—8/15/61	25¢-30¢	15¢-20¢

Description	Unused	Used
STATUE OF LIBERTY SERIES (CONTINUED)		
Statue of Liberty 22¢—7/4/85	35¢-40¢	15¢-20¢
Statue of Liberty 22¢—7/4/86	40¢-45¢	20¢-25¢
The American Legion, Flag & Eagle Veterans As Citizens	20¢-25¢	20¢-25¢
The Birth of Liberty 2¢—4/4/25	$5-$6	$3-$4
The Minute Men 5¢—4/4/25	$18-$20	$11-$13
Torch of Enlightenment 3¢—10/16/40	15¢-20¢	15¢-20¢
United Nations Conference 5¢—4/25/45	15¢-20¢	15¢-20¢
WORLD WARS I AND II SERIES		
Allied Nations 2¢—1/14/43	15¢-20¢	15¢-20¢
Allied Victory 3¢—3/03/19	$9-$10	$3-$4
Deep Red Violet	$1000-$2000	$1000-$1500
Light Reddish Violet	$8-$10	$3-$4
Red Violet	$35-$45	$10-$12
90mm Antiaircraft Gun 2¢—10/16/40	15¢-20¢	15¢-20¢
World War I Veterans 22¢—8/26/85	35¢-40¢	15¢-20¢
Veterans of World War II 3¢—5/9/46	15¢-20¢	15¢-20¢

Statue of Liberty 1¢,
October 16, 1940,
unused 15¢-20¢,
used 15¢-20¢

Allied Victory 3¢, March 3, 1919,
unused $9-$10, used $3-$4

Win the War 3¢,
July 4, 1942,
unused 15¢-20¢,
used 15¢-20¢

Iwo Jima (Marines) 3¢,
July 11, 1945,
unused 15¢-20¢,
used 15¢-20¢

Uncle Sam Items

I couldn't have written this chapter and really had a full understanding of Uncle
Sam and his importance to America, past and present, without first talking to the
foremost collector and authority on Uncle Sam collectibles, Gerald E. Czulewicz,
Sr. Gerald began collecting and researching art as a teenager in his hometown of
Erie, Pennsylvania. This early research began his interest in rare American books and
documents, which led to what would become a lifelong fascination with Americana,
particularly with the image and history of Uncle Sam. This interest resulted in Gerald
seeking out the works of American illustrators and Uncle Sam artists such as Thomas Nast and James Montgomery Flagg. The Uncle Sam costumes used by models
for both Nast and Flagg are among the many unique artifacts that Gerald has acquired, helping to make his collection the largest of its kind in the world. I feel
honored that Gerald helped my writing of this chapter by sharing his knowledge and
understanding of America's favorite uncle—Uncle Sam.

There are many stories about the origin of Uncle Sam and whether or not Uncle
Sam really existed. One of the most published accountings is the story of Samuel
Wilson of Troy, New York. During the War of 1812 and many years following, Samuel
Wilson was a meat packer and a purveyor of goods to the U.S. Army. The crates that
were prepared for shipment were required to be stamped "U.S." As the story goes, the
recipients of these goods began to refer to Samuel Wilson as Uncle Sam since his
initial was on the goods. The other origin was the existence of a Brother Jonathan as
either being the original Uncle Sam or holding the symbolic position of an Uncle

Sam. Whatever the true story is, there is no doubt that the image of Uncle Sam and the message he delivers have stirred the roots of patriotism in America almost since the nation's very beginnings. That Uncle Sam has been and continues to be an integral part of our lives is evidenced by the various items depicted in this chapter.

Balance Game, 1940

"The American Way: Liberty and Justice for All" and "Balance the Scales of Justice," with front depicting Uncle Sam and the Statue of Liberty standing in front of a map of the United States. $100-$125

Banks

★ **Cash Register Bank, Durable Toy and Novelty Company, 1942**
   Uncle Sam's Register Bank, Three Coin, 5-$^7/_8$" x 4-$^1/_2$" x 5-$^1/_8$". $60-$70

★ **Cash Register Bank, Durable Toy and Novelty Company, 1942**
   Uncle Sam's Dime Bank with eagle in gold on top, 4-$^1/_2$" x 3-$^3/_8$". $40-$50

★ **Metal/Cast-Iron Uncle Sam Bank, 1886**
   Full figure of Uncle Sam, with blue umbrella in left hand, which fits into a hole on the base of the bank. A red suitcase by right foot is labeled "U.S." Red base of the bank pictures the American eagle with a blue banner reading "Uncle Sam" above it. $4500-$6500

★ **Tin Hat Uncle Sam Bank, 1952**
   Red, white, and blue metal Uncle Sam hat, 3-$^1/_4$" x 3-$^1/_4$" x 4-$^1/_8$". $50-$60

★ **Uncle Sam Ceramic Bank, 1941**
   Red, white, and blue bust figure of Uncle Sam holding a banner reading "For My Income Tax," 7" x 4-$^3/_4$". $50-$60

★ **Uncle Sam Semiporcelain Bank, 1898**
   White with gold hat band, 4-$^1/_8$" x 3-$^1/_4$". $125-$150

Bookmark (Silk), 1898

"United We Stand [picture of Uncle Sam] Welcome Home." $50-$60

Bumper Ornament, 1936

"Drive Ahead with Roosevelt," picture of Uncle Sam with hands on the shoulder of Franklin D. Roosevelt, die-cut molded with gold, red, white, and dark blue paint, manufactured by ARPO, New York, 8" x 11-$^1/_4$". $150-$175

Chocolate Mold, 1890

Heavy metal Uncle Sam mold with "No. 514" on his back and "S & Co." on the front of his hat, 5" x 3". $40-$160

Bicycle Act, American Flyer Toy Company, 1915, $100-$125; Yankee Sand Mill sand toy, 1908, $400-$500; dancing Uncle Sam, 1885, $3,000-$3,500

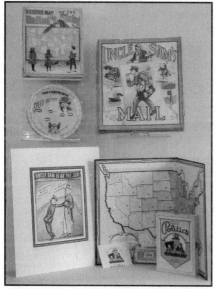

Board games: Uncle Sam's Mail, Milton Bradley Company, 1910, 16-¼" x 15" x 1-¼", $500-$600; Game of Politics, Parker Brothers, 1950, 17" x 19-¼", $70-$80; jigsaw puzzle—dissected map of the United States, 1890, $400-$500; Game-Disk-O-Knowledge, 1942, $200-300; "Uncle Sam Is On the Job" poster, 1942, $225-$250

Christmas Tree Ornament, 1994
Mouth-blown and hand-painted glass ornament with picture of Uncle Sam, produced by Christopher Radko (Limited Edition). $25-$35

Christmas Tree Ornaments, 1918
Four Uncle Sam cutout Christmas tree ornaments, 4" x 1". $50-$60

Cookie Jar, 1973
Uncle Sam's hat. $200-$300

Creamer. Ridgway Sterling Pottery, Lawley, England, 1909
Uncle Sam's face influenced by image of Abraham Lincoln, 3-¼" x 2-¼". $90-$110

Doll. Uncle Sam Papier-Mâché Figure, Unger Doll and Toy Company, 1890–1893
Striped pants, blue coat, red vest, blue hat with stars on band, on blue base. $250-$300

Doll. Uncle Sam Plastic and Rubber Doll, Fun World Inc., 1948
Red and white striped pants, blue jacket, white shirt, and red bow tie on black plastic stand. $60-$75

Doorstop, 1900
Uncle Sam cast-iron doorstop with original paint, 14" x 6-½" x 4". $300-$400

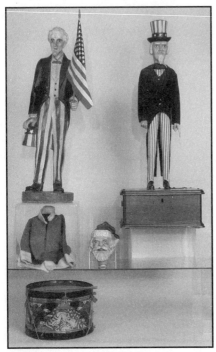

Flag holder figurine, 1930, 28" x 8-½" diameter, $500-$600; Uncle Sam/Santa Claus automation window display for Macy's Department Store, New York, 1917, rare, $6000-$9000; Uncle Sam drum, 1914, metal drum with leather skin, rope binders, wood rims, 10-⅞" diameter, $200-$250

Ink Blotter, 1932
Uncle Sam praying, superimposed over picture of Abraham Lincoln and Valley Forge, 5" x 3-³/₈". $25-$30

Ink Blotter. Edwin C. Price & Company, 1942
Picture of Uncle Sam pointing his finger saying, "I Want Your Waste Paper," 3-¹/₂" x 5-¹/₄". $10-$15

Jigsaw Puzzle. United States with Uncle Sam, Milton Bradley Company, 1890
Full-colored map of the United States, chromolithograph on paper mounted on wood, 9-³/₄" x 14-¹/₄". $400-$500

Lamp, 1950
Uncle Sam standing by U.S. flag with "Pledge of Allegiance" plaque, plastic and portable, 7-⁷/₈" x 4-³/₈" x 4". $50-$60

Paint Set. The American Brilliant Paints, American Crayon Company, 1943
Picture of Uncle Sam dressed as soldier marching with children, 4-⁵/₈" x 5-⁷/₈". $60-$75

Paint Set, 1942
Red box with picture of Uncle Sam, 8-¹/₂" x 5-¹/₄". $90-$100

Pencil Box. Ozark Pencil Company, St. Louis, Missouri, 1918
Paper on wood with picture of Uncle Sam, Tin top, 12" x 1 ¹/₄". $75-$85

Pencil Sharpener. Ever-Sharp Manufacturing Company, New York, 1918
Cast pot-metal standing figure of Uncle Sam walking, copper-plated finish. $125-$150

Pennant, 1919 (World War I)
"Welcome Home" and "Well Done My Boys," Uncle Sam amid the stars with his arms around two military personnel, 25-¹/₄" x 10-³/₄". $90-$115

Pitcher. Ridgway Sterling Pottery, Lawley, England, 1909
Uncle Sam's face influenced by image of Abraham Lincoln, 11-^{1}/$_4$" x 7". $175-$195

Playing Cards, 1953
James Montgomery Flagg's "I Want You" depicted on back of cards. $12-$15

Puzzle. Uncle Sam United States Map Puzzle, Milton Bradley, 1914
Full-color chromolithograph puzzle. Front is map of the United States, reverse is the United States Capitol Building with 36 of allied countries. Very rare. $350-$450

Salt Shaker, 1920
Pair of hand-painted Uncle Sam salt shakers, 2-^{1}/$_8$" x 1-^{1}/$_2$". $35-$40

Serving Plate, 1950
Semi-porcelain plate with 24K gold-plated, scalloped edge, large picture of Uncle Sam in middle surrounded by smaller Uncle Sams. $40-$50

Smoking Pipe, 1890
Hand-carved and painted hard-wood image of Uncle Sam with ebony stem, 2-^{1}/$_8$" x 6-^{1}/$_4$". $250-$275

Stamp Machine. Automatic Dispenser Co., Los Angeles, California, 1945
Automatic stamp machine with Uncle Sam picture in center, nickel and dime slots, 20-^{1}/$_2$" x 7-^{7}/$_8$" x 4-^{1}/$_4$", Serial No. 4819. $100-$150

Uncle Sam Suit, 1870
Original Uncle Sam suit used by Thomas Nast for his model with Harper's Publishing Company. $20,000+

Uncle Sam dolls: wax doll, 1900, $1200-$1500; papier-mâché figure, $250-$300; Uncle Sam doll with bisque head, 1892, $2500-$3000; composition doll, 1892, $250-$275; figure bisque, 1870, $300-$350

Uncle Sam Strength Tester, Caille Company, 1908, "Shake With Uncle Sam," cast-metal bust of Uncle Sam mounted on oak cabinet with cast-iron paw feet, originally cost one cent, $25,000-$30,000

Uncle Sam Suit and Top Hat, 1916

Worn by James Montgomery Flagg while using himself as a model for the original painting of the first "I Want You" poster. This original suit was also used by Flagg while producing the very first "I Want You" images for *Leslie's Weekly* magazine cover art on July 6, 1916, and February 15, 1917. $30,000+

Uncle Sam Patriotic Artwork and Prints

S ome of the most important and expensive artwork in this category are the original works by James Montgomery Flagg, owing to their rarity and the difficulty in locating his work. While there were other well-known artists who also used the image of Uncle Sam, Flagg's images are considered the best and most notable works of art. In part this is due to his famous "I Want You" 1917 World War I recruiting poster. As with the artwork, numerous prints and engravings by various artists were produced in the 19th and 20th centuries depicting Uncle Sam in many forms and connected to many events. A note of caution: The serious collector of this artwork should always acquire proper authenticity when purchasing these items.

"About Time To Get To Work," 1897
"War with Spain," Uncle Sam reading newspaper and reaching for rifle, 15-^{1}/$_2$" x 11-^{1}/$_2$", artist: Homer C. Davenport. $75-$100

"All Nations Are Welcome to the World's Columbian Exposition Chicago," 1893
Uncle Sam welcoming all the nations, color plate print, copyright J. M. Campbell, 7-^{1}/$_4$" x 12". $125-$150

"A Belated Inspection," ca. 1899
Uncle Sam holding cannon swab looking down cannon that reads "Armament Industry," crayon and charcoal, 14-^{1}/$_4$" x 14-^{1}/$_4$", artist: Jonathan Cassell. $3000-$4500

"Come On America, We've Got A Big Job To Do!" 1918, 24" x 20", artist: James Montgomery Flagg, $18,000-$20,000

"Black Uncle Sam," ca. 1885
Black Uncle Sam selling cigars, 16" x 12", artist: unknown. Rare. $1200-$1500

"Cuba—Go 'Way. I Don't Like You," ca. 1901
Political cartoon of Uncle Sam being pushed away by little boy with hat that reads "Cuba," pen and ink, 20" x 18", artist: Alexander VanLeshout. $2000-$2500

"Flying Uncle Sam," 1928
Norman Rockwell painting of Uncle Sam flying with airplanes, drawn for the 1928 cover of *The Saturday Evening Post*, 13-$^1/_2$" x 10-$^1/_2$". $150-$200

"Gentlemen, Our Country," 1916
Uncle Sam pointing to flag and holding hat, Morris & Bendien, 10" x 8". $50-$60

"Get Behind Uncle Sam, Buy War Savings Stamps," ca. 1917–1918
Uncle Sam with rifle over his shoulder, being patted on back, words on sleeve of hand read "W.S.S.," pen, ink, and watercolor, 30" x 21", artist: William Henry Walker. $7000-$9000
Original art work for World War I poster.

"Home from the War," 1918, pen and ink, 18-$^1/_2$" x 13-$^1/_2$", artist: James Montgomery Flagg, $12,000-$15,000

"Getting The Old Gun Ready," 1897
"Spanish American War," Uncle Sam cleaning his rifle, 15-$^1/_2$" x 11-$^1/_2$", artist: Homer C. Davenport. $75-$90

"He Is Your Uncle Sam," 1918
Uncle Sam standing with sleeves rolled up. "The Story of what Uncle Sam stands for" by Frederic J. Haskin, 9" x 6". $10-$15

"I Need You Again," 1952
Picture of Uncle Sam saying "Your Army and Your Air Force Serve the Nation and Mankind in War and Peace," 13" x 9-$^3/_4$", artist: James Montgomery Flagg. $20-$25

"I need You *Now!*" 1952, watercolor, 26" x 28", artist: James Montgomery Flagg, $21,000-$24,000

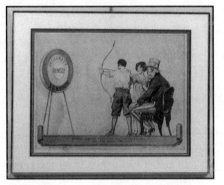

"Integrity, Honesty, Service," 1917, watercolor, 18-½" x 23-½", artist: James Montgomery Flagg, $20,000-$22,000

"I Need Your Skill In A War Job," 1944
Uncle Sam pointing finger, 28" x 20", artist: James Montgomery Flagg. $125-$150

"I Want You For the U.S. Army, Nearest Recruiting Station," ca. 1944
Uncle Sam pointing, with stern look on face, oil painting on canvas, 17' x 10', artist: James Montgomery Flagg. $3000-$4000
Three-section oil painting used during World War II for the Brooklyn, New York, Recruiting Center.

"Lindbergh," 1928
Charles Lindbergh dressed as Uncle Sam along with a poem, "Our Brave Lindy," by Elsie J. Miller, 12" x 9", artist: James Stuart. $40-$50

"The Love of Freedom," 1917
Uncle Sam waving American flag attached to rifle, full-color lithograph, 19-¹/₂" x 15-¹/₂", artist: Ezio Anichini, Florence, Italy. $150-$200

"More Parade, For More Patriotic Enthusiasm," 1942
Uncle Sam leading victory parade along with Miss Liberty and Franklin D. Roosevelt, followed by soldier and factory workers. A little boy who is watching is saying, "Mommy! Where's all the funny clowns?" and mother replies, "This is no circus son, this is the 1942 all out for victory parade!" Pen, ink, and watercolors, 9-¹/₂" x 13", artist: Silas Olson. $400-$450
Political drawing for the Minneapolis Star and Tribune.

"Pershing in France Berlin or Bust," 1917
Uncle Sam and General Pershing in France watching troops, full-color rotagravier, 20-¹/₂" x 15", artist: E. G. Renesch. $200-$250

"Political Chestnuts," ca. 1887
Uncle Sam looking up into chestnut tree, holding the figures of Andersen, O'Brien, and Grant, Donohue and Quintard "chestnuts" are on the ground, pen and ink, 20" x 15", artist: C. deGrimm. $1500-$2000
Cover illustration for magazine publication *Political Chestnuts*.

"Rollin' 'em Up!" ca. 1917
Plaster production piece flag holder depicting Uncle Sam rolling up his sleeves, with determined look, 12-^{5}/$_8$" high, 3-^{1}/$_2$" x 3-^{5}/$_8$" base, hole in left rear of base to hold the flag. $400-$450
Commissioned by F. W. Eichorn in 1917 for use in storefront window display during World War I. Model executed by sculptor Guido Rebechini (signed on base). Copyright 1917 by F. W. Eichorn on back of base.

"The Spirit of 1943," 1943
Comprehensive oil sketch of Uncle Sam rolling up his sleeves, standing over a railroad yard with trains, tanks, and background of industrial factories, oil painting on "stat" paper mounted on board, 16-^{1}/$_2$" x 23", artist: Dean Cornwell. $3000-$3500
Commissioned by the Pennsylvania Railroad and reproduced in *The Saturday Evening Post* in 1943 advertisement.

"The Spirit of '76," 1876
Original painting of "The Spirit of '76," artist: Archibald M. Willard. $1.5M–20M (estimate)

"Springfield to Washington, Lincoln vs. Douglas Democrats," Greve Lithographic Company, 1892
Uncle Sam traveling on donkey, 24" x 19", artist: Archibald M. Willard. $1000-$1200

"This Country Must Not Succumb To The Conditions Which Produced Dictators In Europe—President Roosevelt," ca. 1940
Uncle Sam pounding on a table and quoting President Franklin D. Roosevelt, Wolff pencil on coquille board, 13-^{1}/$_4$" x 10-^{3}/$_4$", artist: Rollin Kirby. $700-$900

"Uncle Sam," ca. 1898
Uncle Sam with mean look, rolling up his sleeves, with fist clenched, pen and ink, 20-^{3}/$_4$" x 15-^{3}/$_4$", artist: Ole May. $2300-$2500
Original illustration for the *Washington Post*.

"Uncle Sam," August 17, 1901

Uncle Sam balancing three balls that read "Total Exports July $109,031,158," "Total Exports Seven Months $830,883,816," and "Excess Exports $324,526,625," with man watching whose big stomach reads "The Earth," pen and ink, 22-5/8" x 17-5/8", artist: C. J. Newman. $2000-$2500

"Uncle Sam," 1994, oil painting, 18" x 14", artist: Robert Gunn, $4000-$5000. Original cover art for *Working*

"You Want <u>Me</u>!" May 1960, watercolor, 14" x 10", artist: James Montgomery Flagg, $7,000-$9,000; "Alert," 1941, watercolor, 11" x 8-½", artist: James Montgomery Flagg, $8,000-$10,000. Note: The image of Uncle Sam in "You Want <u>Me</u>!" was the very last image executed by Flagg.

"Uncle Sam," ca. 1988

Uncle Sam within shield with background of stars and stripes, pen, ink, and watercolor, artist: Gerald E. Czulewicz, Sr. $600-$900

"We're On Our Way," American Legion Calendar, 1988

Uncle Sam with sleeves rolled up, surrounded by planes, tanks, and factories, 10-1/4" x 8-1/4", artist: Newell Convers Wyeth. $5-$10 Original art done ca. 1941.

"We've Made a Monkey Out of You," 1943

Uncle Sam with grinder box making a monkey that looks like Hitler dance, Capitol in background, 20" x 15", artist: J. H. King. $200-$250

"Yankee Doodle," 1876

Black and white stone lithograph of Uncle Sam carrying boots, 13-1/2" x 10", artist: Edward Harrison May. $1000-$1200

"You Want <u>Me</u>!" May 1960

Uncle Sam pointing to himself with a serious face, Watercolor. $7000-$9000

This image of Uncle Sam was known to be the very last executed by James Montgomery Flagg shortly before is death.

Military and Red Cross Posters: World Wars I and II

I can't imagine anyone viewing a World War I or II military or Red Cross poster and not saying, "Wow." You don't have to be a war enthusiast, a Red Cross supporter, or an art collector to enjoy and appreciate the colorful graphics, bold images, and exacting artwork of these posters. Even today, looking at one of these posters still brings about deep passions of patriotism, knowing that World Wars I and II introduced America to a big world and a new way of living. What was important about these posters was that, since they could be located anywhere and were highly visible, they rapidly became an immediate, powerful tool that increased recruitment in the Armed Forces, promoted the buying of war bonds and stamps, and supported other important fund-raising endeavors to help the war effort. Above all, these posters evoked a deep feeling of patriotism and hard feelings toward the enemy.

The themes of these posters covered a wide variety of subjects such as national symbols that included American flags and eagles, soldiers in the trenches, Navy ships at sea, and the Statue of Liberty. These posters ultimately influenced and awakened new emotions, attitudes, and feelings about the entire world.

"Be A U.S. Marine!" Broad & Genesse Streets, Utica, New York, 1918, 28" x 40", artist: James Montgomery Flagg, $400-$500

"Gee!! I Wish I Were A Man—I'd Join the Navy," 1003 Main Street, Hartford, 1917, 26" x 40", $700-$800

World War I

"The First Three, Give Till It Hurts, They Gave Till They Died," 1917
Red Cross poster and bond poster with picture of three soldiers who were the first American victims of World War I above red cross. $100-$125

"Flag Of Freedom," 1917
Picture of an Army Corps nurse holding flag, Statue of Liberty and ships in background, soldiers marching off to war, 15-³/₄" x 11-³/₄". $100-$125

"Get in the Game With Uncle Sam," 1917, 19" x 25", J. C. Leyendecker, rare, $1500-$2000

"Give It Your Best," Division of Information, Office for Emergency Management, 1942
Poster of American flag reading "Give It Your Best," 28" x 40". $75-$100

"The Greatest Mother In The World," 1918
Picture of Red Cross nurse looking tired, 20" x 27-¹/₂". $125-$150

"Oh, Boy! That's The Girl—The Salvation Army Lassie—Keep Her On The Job, United War Work Campaign, Nov. 11–18, 1918," 1918
Young boy pointing to Salvation Army woman worker, 30" x 40". $150-$200

"If You Want To Fight, Join The Marines," 1915–1918, 30" x 40", $900-$1200

"I Want You for The Navy," 1917, 26-½" x 40", $700-$800

"Some Backing! The Empire State Needs Soldiers, Join The New York State Guard," 1917
Uncle Sam standing behind American Revolution and World War I soldier, 42" x 30", artist: James Montgomery Flagg. $1200-$1500

"Stand By The Boys In The Trenches, Mine More Coal, United States Fuel Administration," 1918
Picture of soldier and coal miner, 20" x 30". $75-$100

"I Want You For U.S. Army," 1917, 30" x 40", $2500-$3000

"Make Our American Red Cross In Peace As in War," 1919, 19-½" x 30", $125-$150

"The Motor Corps of America,"
1918, 29-¼" x 42-½",
$1200-$1500

"Red Cross Appeal," 1918, 28" x 23",
$400-$500

"The Spirit of America, Join,"
1918, 20" x 29-¼", $600-$800

"Teufel Hundren, German Nickname For U.S. Marines, Devil Dog Recruiting Station," 1918
Marine bulldog chasing dog with German helmet, 20" x 30". $200-$300

"Third Red Cross Roll Call," 1918
Picture of angelic Red Cross volunteer opening her arms to appeal to men and women, 20" x 30". $100-$125

"Uncle Sam Needs That Extra Shovelful, Help Uncle Sam To Win The War," 1917–1918
Uncle Sam standing behind factory worker shoveling coal into furnace, 20" x 28". $75-$100

"War Clouds Gather—'Manhood Willing But Unarmed'—Help The Navy, Join The Navy League Local Headquarters," 1918
Young sailor blowing bugles by U.S. flag, 19" x 28". $250-$350

World War II

"Avenge December 7," 1942
Angry sailor showing fist, 27" x 41". $110-$135

"Don't Get Hurt, It May Cost His Life, War Department Safety Council," 1943
Man with arm in sling over dead soldier, 22" x 28". $125-$150

"Help China! China Is Helping Us, United China Relief," 1938
Uncle Sam helping Chinese refugees, 30" x 20", artist: James Montgomery Flagg.
$300-$400

"The Marines Have Landed!" City Hall, Wilkes-Barre, Pennsylvania, 1942, 26" x 37", artist: James Montgomery Flagg, $250-$350

"He's <u>Sure</u> To Get V-Mail, Safest Overseas Mail," 1943
Soldier holding letter, 22" x 28". $100-$125

"I'm Counting On You! Don't Discuss: Troop Movements, Ship Sailings, War Equipment," 1943
Picture of Uncle Sam with finger over lips, 28" x 20", artist: Leon Helguera. $150-$175

"I Want <u>You</u> For The U.S. Army, Enlist Now," 1941
Picture of Uncle Sam pointing, 40" x 28", artist: James Montgomery Flagg. $500-$600

"Keep 'em Flying! Presented By The United States Army Recruiting Service," 1941
Soldier with face of Uncle Sam in background, 20" x 30". $125-$150

"Let's Finish The Job, Urgent, Experienced Seamen Needed, Merchant Marine, Washington, D.C.," 1943
Sailor at helm of ship, 22" x 28". $125-$150

"Volunteer For Victory, Offer Your Services To Your Red Cross," 1943
Picture of female in blue uniform and cape with Red Cross flags in background, 11" x 14". $65-$85

"We Can't Win A War Without Teamwork On The Battlefield—And On The Home Front, Too!" 1944
Soldier in combat looking through range-finder, 20" x 27". $75-$100

"We Can! We Will! We Must! All effort. All production. All possessions. Brain power. Horse power. Everything channeled in one drive to one goal—VICTORY! Let's work harder at our jobs and do them better." 1942

Uncle Sam rolling up his sleeves in front of factory workers, 39-^{1}/$_2$" x 19", artist: J. W. Schlaikjer. $125-$150

"Want *Action*? Join The U.S. Marine Corps!" 1942, 30" x 40", $350-$450

"We Have Just Begun To Fight! Pearl Harbor, Bataan, Coral Sea, Midway, Guadalcanal, New Guinea, Bismarck Sea, Casablanca, Algiers, Tunisia," 1943

Soldier with M-1 rifle in hand leading the charge, 27" x 41". $90-$120

". . . We Here Highly Resolve That These Dead Shall Not Have Died In Vain . . . REMEMBER DEC. 7th," 1942

Picture of tattered U.S. flag at half-mast, 27" x 41". $90-$120

"Your Duty Ashore . . . His Afloat, Spars, Apply Nearest Coast Guard Office," 1944

Picture of female enlisted Coast Guard sailor with field glasses and sailor with rifle in background, 27" x 41". $250-$300

"Your Red Cross Needs You," 1943

Uncle Sam with nurse and red cross in background, 21" x 14", artist: James Montgomery Flagg. $250-$300

Savings Bonds and Stamps Posters: World Wars I and II

W hile World War I began the need for war bonds and stamps to raise billions of dollars for that war effort, the onset of World War II resulted in our government having to build and maintain an armed force that could win a war, requiring that billions of dollars worth of war bonds and stamps be sold for an indefinite period of time. In order to accomplish this huge task, the War Advertising Council and the War Finance Committee devised and produced an aggressive and far-reaching advertising plan with the daunting task of selling billions of dollars worth of war bonds and stamps while contributing to the morale of all America.

The war bond campaign ultimately became a mixture of passions of national patriotism and a new approach on how consumers spent their dollars. As a result of this advertising campaign, the government enlisted the aid of some of America's most talented and best-known artists such as James Montgomery Flagg, who was responsible for the most famous poster, a serious-looking Uncle Sam pointing and saying "I Want You." These colorful and dramatic savings bonds and stamps posters evoked the patriotic passions of Americans then and still continue to keep our passion alive today in the aftermath of the events of September 11, 2001. By the end of World War II, a total of $157 billion had been raised by a series of eight war bond loan drives.

World War I

"The A.E.F. To The President, 4th Liberty Loan," 1918
Soldier standing next to letter written to president. $100-$150

"American All, Victory Liberty Loan," 1919
Image of glowing Liberty lady holding a laurel wreath to symbolize victory for the people of ethnic backgrounds, 26-³/₄" x 40". $550-$650

"The First Three!" 1918.
20" x 30", $200-$250

"Before Sunset, Buy A U.S. Government Bond Of The 2nd Liberty Loan Of 1917," 1917
Picture of Statue of Liberty, 20" x 30". $200-$250

"Bonds—Which?" 1917
Image of Uncle Sam with shackles labeled "Prussia" in one hand and a Liberty Bond in the other, 14" x 22". $40-$60

"Boys and Girls! You Can Help Your Uncle Sam Win The War, Save Your Quarters, Buy War Savings Stamps," 1917
Uncle Sam holding a young girl with a young boy standing in front of him, 30" x 20", artist: James Montgomery Flagg. $400-$500

"Clear The Way !! Buy Bonds, Fourth Liberty Bond," 1918
Picture of young girl with U.S. flag above sailors firing from deck of ship, 23" x 33-¼". $300-$400

"Fight Or Buy Bonds, Third Liberty Loan," 1917
Beautiful woman draped in white waves an American flag while gesturing to the troops marching, 20" x 30". $500-$600

"For This [picture of Uncle Sam] I Give You This, Buy War Savings Stamps," 1917
Uncle Sam showing how $4 can become $5, 20" x 30", artist: James Montgomery Flagg. $300-$400

"V Invest," 1918, 19-½" x 29-½", $50-$100

"Have You Bought Your Bond? Liberty Loan," 1917
Picture of Statue of Liberty, 21" x 26". $150-$200

"I Am Telling You, On June 28th I Expect You To Enlist In The Army Of War Savers To Back Up My Army Of Fighters, W.S.S. Enlistment," 1918
Picture of Uncle Sam with hand on hips, promoting War Savings Stamps (W.S.S.), 20" x 30", artist: James Montgomery Flagg. $250-$350

"Lend The Way They Fight, Buy Bonds To Your Utmost," 1918
Tattered, heroic doughboy flinging a grenade into a foxhole as enemy soldiers huddle below, 27-¹/₂" x 41-¹/₂". $150-$200

"Must Children Die and Mothers Plead in Vain? Buy More Liberty Bonds," 1918
Poster is a stark image of war, suffering children, and desperate mothers, 30" x 40". $250-$300

"Over The Top For You, Buy U.S. Gov't Bonds, Third Liberty Loan," 1918

"The Road to Berlin – He Is Building It – He Needs Your Help – Look Him In The Eyes And Then Buy All Of The Liberty Bonds You Can," 1917
Soldier with a cheerful grin making an appeal, 20" x 24". $75-$100

"My Soldier, How Can You Help?" 1918, 14" x 21", $50-$65; "Stamp! Stamp! Stamp! The Boys are Marching," 1918, 13-½" x 18-½", $50-$65

"Our Daddy is fighting at the Front for <u>You</u>—Back him up— Buy a United States Gov't Bond of the 2nd Liberty Loan of 1917," 1917, 20" x 30", $125-$175

"'Shall We Be More Tender With Our Dollars Than With The Lives Of Our Sons?' (MacCadoo, Secretary Of Treasury), Buy A United States Government Bond Of The 2nd Liberty Loan Of 1917," 1917
Picture of Uncle Sam in front of soldiers marching and ships at sea, 20" x 30", artist: Dan Sayre Groesbeck. $300-$400

"Sure! We'll Finish The Job – Victory Liberty Loan," 1918
Factory worker reaching deep into his pockets, 26" x 38". $100-$150

"That Liberty Shall Not Perish From The Earth – Buy Liberty Bonds – Fourth Liberty Loan," 1918
Statue of Liberty watching America under attack, 30" x 40". $400-$500

"U.S.A. Bonds – Third Liberty Campaign – Boy Scouts Of America – Weapons For Liberty," 1918
Picture of woman dressed like Statue of Liberty holding shield, a Boy Scout on one knee handing a sword to the woman, 20" x 30". $400-$500

"Victory Bonds Will Help Stop This," 1918 (Canadian)
Commemorating sinking of the hospital ship *Llandovery Castle* by German U-boats, 24" x 36". $125-$150

World War II

"Bring him home Sooner! BUY WAR BONDS," 1942, 22" x 28", $125-$165

"Appreciate America – Everybody Pull Together – Buy United States War Bonds and Savings Stamps," 1943
Uncle Sam rowing in a boat, 22" x 16", artist: James Montgomery Flagg. $250-$300

"Back the Attack, Buy War Bonds, 3rd War Loan," 1943
Soldier with rifle, parachutes in background, 10" x 14". $100-$150

"Beware Of The Wrath Of A Patient Man— Keep Your War Savings Pledge," 1938
Uncle Sam with hands on hips, looking serious, 30" x 20", artist: James Montgomery Flagg. $300-$400

"Buy Now For The Bigger 7th War Loan," 1943, 27" x 41", $90-$125

"Keep him flying! BUY WAR BONDS," 1944, 20" x 28", $175-$200

"Buy War Bonds," 1942
Uncle Sam in clouds, holding American flag, with fighter planes in the sky and soldiers on the ground. $200-$300
First poster produced by the U.S. government.

"Combat America – Produced and Narrated By Major Clark Gable For The U.S. Army Air Forces – Buy Extra War Bonds," 1944
Picture of Major Clark Gable in aviator uniform, 27" x 41". $400-$700

"Save Freedom Of Speech," 1943, 30" x 40", artist: Norman Rockwell, $350-$450

"Help Bring Them Back To You! Find Time For War Work – Raise And Share Food – Walk and Carry Packages – Conserve Everything You Have – Save 10% in War Bonds – Make Yours A Victory Home," 1943
Picture of home with a banner with one star and sign that reads "This is A Victory 'V' Home," 22" x 28". $85-$100

"Let's All Fight – Buy War Bonds," 1942
Soldier attacking with rifle and bayonet, U.S. Printing Office, 22" x 28". $125-$150

"Save Freedom Of Worship,"
1943, 30" x 40", $300-$400

"Let's Give Him Enough And On Time," 1942
Graphic painting of soldier with ragged uniform
shooting a machine gun, artist: Norman Rockwell.
$250-$350
More than 25,000 of these posters were printed
for display in factories.

"Next! 6th War Loan," 1944
Picture of soldier looking at island of Japan,
22" x 28". $125-$165

**"Right Behind Him – With What It Takes to
Haul What He Needs – Buy Defense Stamps
and Bonds Now – Association Of American
Railroads,"** 1943
Picture of soldier with rifle, standing in front of
train, 20" x 28". $65-$75

"The Sky's The Limit! Keep Buying War Bonds," 1944
Men and women factory workers working on airplane, 20" x 27". $50-$60

**"They're Fighting Harder Than Ever – Are You Buying MORE WAR BONDS
Than Ever?"** 1943
Charging soldiers with tank in background and yelling helmeted soldier in fore-
ground, U.S. Treasury Department, 20" x 28". $175-$225

"This Home Did It Again, 6th War Loan,"
1944, $100-$125

"To Have and to Hold!" 1944,
20" x 28", $175-$225

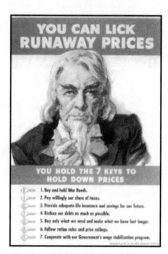

"You Can Lick Runaway Prices,"
1950, 24" x 18", $100-$125

"This Year Give A Share In America – Buy Defense Bonds and Stamps," 1944
Picture of smiling Santa Claus. $75-$100

"You Buy 'Em – We'll Fly 'Em – Defense Bonds – Stamps," 1942
Pilot in cockpit of fighter plane, U.S. Treasury Department, 20" x 28". $200-$250

Collectors

United States

Alabama

Steve Holland
(Bottles)
1740 Serene Drive
Birmingham, AL 35215
(205) 853-7929

Matt Lippa
(Folk Art)
P.O. Box 256
Mentone, AL 35984
(256) 634-4037

Marcia Weber
(Folk Art)
1050 Woodley Road
Montgomery, AL 36106
(334) 262-5349

Arizona

Lois Cordey
(Sheet Music)
5623 North 64th Avenue
Glendale, AZ 85301
(623) 931-2835

Michael and Karen Miller
(Bottles)
9214 West Gary Road
Peoria, AZ 85345
(602) 277-0433

Bryan Grapentine
(Bottles and Advertising)
1939 West Waltann Lane
Phoenix, AZ 85023
(602) 993-9757

Arkansas

Don and Jackie Leonard
(Bottles)
1118 Green Mt. Drive
Little Rock, AR 72211
(501) 224-5432

California

Mike Prero
(Matchbook Covers)
12659 Eckard Way
Auburn, CA 95603-3516
Fax (978) 389-0396

Talbert Kanigher
(Movie Posters)
P.O. Box 6294
Burbank, CA 91505-6294
(818) 848-6469

Susan Cox
(Matchbook Covers)
800 Murray Drive
El Cajon, CA 92020
(619) 697-5922

Lee Aronsohn
(Postcards)
16430 Westfall Place
Encino, CA 91436
(818) 905-0225

Trudy Prescott
(Movie Memorabilia)
2791-F North Texas Street, Suite 112
Fairfield, CA 94533

Harry Lemay, LeMay Movie Posters
P.O. Box 480879
Los Angeles, CA 90048
(323) 935-4053

Ken Taylor
(Posters)
11661 San Vicente, #3304
Los Angeles, CA 90049
(310) 442-0054

Ed Kuskie
(Bottles)
27465 Sereno
Mission Viejo, CA 92691
(949) 597-2165

Lynn Wenzel
(Sheet Music)
15134 Airport Road
Nevada City, CA 95959
(530) 470-0360

Brent Gutekunst
(Stamps)
P.O. Box 6289
Newport Beach, CA 92658
(949) 567-1234

Peter Gwillim Kreitler
(Magazines, July 1942)
1011 Swarthmore Avenue, #4
Pacific Palisades, CA 90272
(310) 230-2200

David Kneubuhl,
Movie Memories Poster Shop
(Movie Posters)
502 Waverly Street
Palo Alto, CA 94301
(650) 328-6265

Lewis Baer
(Postcards)
P.O. Box 621
Penngrove, CA 94951
(707) 795-2650

Mel and Barbara De Mello
(Advertising)
P.O. Box 186
Pollock Pines, CA 95726
(916) 644-6133

Roger Baker
(Advertising Items)
P.O. Box 620417
Redwood, CA 94062-0417
(650) 851-7188

Vivian Briggs
(Political Items)
4443 Linwood Place
Riverside, CA 92506
(909) 781-3121

James Yeaw
(Stamps)
P.O. Box 1077
Rocklin, CA 95677
(916) 624-7281

Thom March, Movie Memories
(Movie Posters)
P.O. Box 660541
Sacramento, CA 95825
(916) 921-5016

Ada Fitzsimmons
(Postcards)
P.O. Box 337
San Anselmo, CA 94979
(415) 454-5552

Ralf Mulhern
3710 Alabama Street, Apt. #24
San Diego, CA 92104-3344
donnamulhern@juno.com

Martin Jacobs
(World War II items, 1941–1945)
P.O. Box 22026
San Francisco, CA 94122-0026
(415) 661-7552

Richard Simon
(Stamps)
220 Bush Street, Suite 1600
San Francisco, CA 94104
(415) 392-1010

Garrison Dover,
Pacific Posters International
(Posters)
P.O. Box 3896
Santa Barbara, CA 93130
(805) 682- 2713

Derek Abrams
(Bottles)
129 East El Camino
Santa Maria, CA 93454
(805) 922-4208

Scott Weiss
(Movie Memorabilia)
1158 26th, #489
Santa Monica, CA 90403
(310) 442-0040

Steve Schmale
(Postcards)
2231 Creekside Road
Santa Rosa, CA 95404
(707) 838-1859

Ben Weed
(Flags)
P.O. Box 4643
Stockton, CA 95204
B.K.Weed@worldnet.att.net

Steve Neis
(Postcards)
P.O. Box 1915
Temple City, CA 91780
(253) 851-9964

Ed Anderson
(Postcards)
P.O. Box 1915
Temple City, CA 91780
(626) 309-7545

Roger Pearce
(Stamps)
545 North Mountain Avenue, Suite 109
Upland, CA 91786
(909) 861-9547

Diana Douglas and Michael Ogle
American Garage
(Folk Art)
6545 Costello Avenue
Van Nuys, CA 91401
(818) 989-7474

Neil Austinson
(Advertising Items)
P.O. Box 1691
Windsor, CA 95492-1692
(707) 837-9685

Christopher Perry
(Movie Memorabilia)
7470 Church Street, Suite A
Yucca Valley, CA 92284
(760) 365-0475

Colorado

Earl F. Dodge
(Political Items)
P.O. Box 2635
Denver, CO 80201
(303) 572-0646

Dave Cheadle
(Advertising Items)
3706 South Acoma Street
Englewood, CO 80110
(303) 761-7906

Connecticut

Laurel Kane
(Postcards)
148 Old Kings Highway North
Darien, CT 06820
(203) 655-3893

Barbara and Ricard DePalma
(Postcards)
609 Kent Road, Route 7
Gaylordsville, CT 06755
(860) 350-4140

Dave Cunningham
(Stamps, Appraiser)
56 Hubbard Avenue
Stamford, CT 06905
(203) 323-4872

Delaware

Charles Dubsky
(Military Collectibles)
686 North Dupont Blvd, #328
Milford, DE 19963-1002
(302) 422-7766

Florida

Bill Simmons
(Movie Posters)
8955 N.W. 19th Street
Coral Springs, FL 33071-6109
(954) 340-0734

John Zak, III
(Stamps, Appraiser)
437 North Clyde Morris Boulevard
Daytona Beach, FL 32114
(386) 255-4425

Marguerite Cantine
(Postcards)
223 S.E. 37th Avenue
Ocala, FL 34471-3045
(352) 694-4514

Len Ettinger
(Stamps)
3865 Lancewood Drive
Pompano Beach, FL 33065
(954) 344-8106

Georgia

John Gingerich
(Political Items)
P.O. Box 358
Lexington, GA 30648-0358
(706) 743-3420

Roger Burgoon
(Sheet Music)
425 Zetterower Road
Statesboro, GA 30458
(912) 764-3195

Hawaii

Eldon Almquist
(Political Items, Richard M. Nixon)
975 Maunawili Circle
Kailua, HI 96743
(808) 262-9837

Illinois

Roger Harvey
(Postcards)
Postcard Collecting Worldwide
170 Selwyn Lane
Buffalo Grove, IL 60089
(847) 520-8145

Dwight Cleveland
(Movie Posters)
P.O. Box 10922
Chicago, IL 60610
(773) 525-9152

Ken Khuana
(World War I Posters)
155 Harbor Drive, #4812
Chicago, IL 60601-7378
(312) 642-0554

Allan Mellis
(Postcards)
1115 West Montana
Chicago, IL 60614
(773) 327-9123

Robert M. Weisz
(Postcards)
4562 North Austin Avenue
Chicago, IL 60630
(773) 545-2929

Jim Wiemers
(Sheet Music)
5312 Seiler Road
Dorsey, IL 62021-1700
(618) 377-1700

Jerry Abert
(Postcards)
631 Broadway
East Alton, IL 62024
(618) 259-0901

David Yates
(Political Items)
321 West Church Street
Genoa, IL 60135
(815) 784-3369

Frank and Barbara Pollack
(Folk Art)
1214 Green Bay Road
Highland Park, IL 60035
(847) 433-2213

John Stachmus
(World War II Posters)
Rural Route 1, Box 110
Homer, IL 61849
(217) 896-2859

Susan Nicholson
(Postcards)
P.O. Box 595
Lisle, IL 60532
(630) 964-5240

Ronald Krueger
(Movie Posters)
P.O. Box 741
Oak Park, IL 60603
(708) 788-8235

Indiana

Mark Sutton
(Flags)
2035 Saint Andrews Circle
Carmel, IN 46032-9547
(317) 844-5648

Don Beck
(Political Items)
P.O. Box 15305
Fort Wayne, IN 46885-5305
(219) 486-3010

Michael McQuillen
(Political Items)
P.O. Box 50022
Indianapolis, IN 46250
(317) 845-1721

Don Johnson
(Military Collectibles)
5110 South Greensboro Pike
Knightstown, IN 46148-9596
(765) 345-5758

Iowa

Tom Rutledge
(Advertising Items)
3015 Bever Avenue S.E.
Cedar Rapids, IA 52403-3028
(319) 399-1427

Joe Doerring
(Political Items)
P.O. Box 35351
Des Moines, IA 50315
(515) 285-7702

Kansas

Terri McDaniels
(Postcards)
6613 East 47th Street South
Derby, KS 67037

Kentucky

Jerry A. Phelps
(Advertising Items)
1500 Van Buren Road
Mount Eden, KY 40046-9552
(502) 859-4063

Maine

Bob Harvey
(Magazines)
P.O. Box 183
North Sullivan, ME 04664-0183
(207) 422-3083

Maryland

Bob Cereghino
(Political/Advertising Items)
6400 Baltimore National Pike,
Suite 170A-319
Baltimore, MD 21228-3914
(410) 766-7593

Sheldon Lerman
(Political/Historical Items)
7505 Osler Drive
Baltimore, MD 21204-7736
(410) 321-1514

George and Marcella Lorden
(Postcards)
522 South Streeper Street
Baltimore, MD 21224
(410) 675-6098

Richard L. Wilson
(Movie Memorabilia)
3511 Turner Lane
Chevy Chase, MD 20815
(301) 652-4644

Larry Krug
(Political Items, Calvin Coolidge)
18222 Flower Hill Way, #299
Gaithersburg, MD 20879
(301) 926-8663

V. Lee Cox
(Postcards)
Memory Lane Postcards
P.O. Box 66, Keymar, MD 21757
(410) 775-0188

Mary L. Martin Ltd.
(Postcards)
4899 Pulaski Highway
P.O. Box 787
Perrville, MD 21903
(410) 575-7768

Ben Egerton
(Postcards)
13009 Dover Road
Reisterstown, MD 21136-5512
(410) 561-5062

Massachusetts

Mark Suozzi
(Political Items)
P.O. Box 102
Ashfield, MA 01330
(413) 628-3241

Rudy Franchi
(Movie Posters)
51 North Margin Street
Boston, MA 02113
(617) 720-2211

Tony Fusco
(World War II Posters; Author of
The Confident Collector: Identification &
Price Guide to Posters)
1 Murdock Terrace
Brighton, MA 02135-2817
(617) 787-2637

Stuart Katz
(Stamps)
P.O. Box 656
Middleton, MA 01949
(978) 777-2327

Michigan

John Green, Movie Poster Page
(Movie Posters)
2729 Cranbrook Road
Ann Arbor, MI 48104
(734) 973-7303

Ken Hosner
(Political Items)
5692 Comstock
Kalamazoo, MI 49001
(616) 345-5983

Mark McNee
(Advertising Items)
1009 Vassar Drive
Kalamazoo, MI 49001-4483
(616) 343-8393

Michael Hennigan
(Folk Art)
20816 East Eleven Mile
Saint Clair Shores, MI 48081-1565
(313) 822-9730

Minnesota

Gerald Czulewicz
(Uncle Sam Collectibles)
25699 Highway 65 N.E.
Isanti, MN 55040
(763) 444-9216

Paul Bengston
(Political Items)
1225 North Seventh Street
Minneapolis, MN 55411-4060

Pam Brin, Pam Brin Gallery
(Posters)
8 Park Lane
Minneapolis, MN 55416
(612) 920-3030

Cary Demont
(Political/Historical Items)
P.O. Box 16013
Minneapolis, MN 55416
(763) 522-0957

Steve Ketcham
(Advertising Items)
P.O. Box 24114
Minneapolis, MN 55424-0114
(952) 920-4204

Mark Quilling
(Matchbook Covers)
1000 Edgerton Street, #1313
Saint Paul, MN 55101-3958
(651) 772-9398

Missouri

Robert M. Levine
(Political Items)
#2 Troll Court
Ballwin, MO 63011
(636) 394-4370

Trenton Boyd
(Postcards)
P.O. Box 517
Columbia, MO 65205
(573) 882-2461

Jim Taylor
(Postcards)
P.O. Box 399
Neosho, MO 64850
(417) 451-3463

New Hampshire

Norwood Keeney III
(Political/Historical Items)
P.O. Box 1026
Georges Mills, NH 033751-1026
(603) 763-9157

Wayland Bunnell
(Sheet Music)
199 Tarrytown Road
Manchester, NH 03103
(603) 668-5466

New Jersey

Dan Calandriello
(Posters)
10 Weston Place
Eatontown, NJ 07724
(732) 542-4770

Anthony's
(Stamps)
P.O. Box 1523
Englewood Cliffs, NJ 07632
(800) 451-9645

Scott Kitchen
(Stamps)
1301 Sunny Slope Road
Bridgewater, NJ 08807

Don and Pat Pocher
(Postcards)
11 South Lafayette Street
Cape May, NJ 08204
(609) 884-3115

Sandy Marrone
(Sheet Music)
113 Oakwood Drive
Cinnaminson, NJ 08077
(856) 829-6104

Richard D. Hagerman
(Casino Matchcovers)
824 Peachy Canyon Circle, #101
Mount Laurel, NJ 89144
(702) 243-9340

Jacques C. Schiff
(Stamps)
195 Main Street
Ridgefield Park, NJ 07660
(201) 641-5566

Allen Radwill
(Sheet Music)
23 Hunters Lane
Vincentown, NJ 08088
(609) 953-5473

Donald Ackerman
(Political/Historical Items)
P.O. Box 3487
Wallington, NJ 07057
(973) 779-8785

Marc Zydiak
(Movie Posters)
P.O. Box 285
Westfield, NJ 07091
(908) 654-6505

New Mexico

Donald Hardisty
(Postcards)
3020 East Majestic Ridge
Las Cruces, NM 88011
(505) 522-3721

New York

Gene Christian
(Military Collectibles)
3849 Bailey Avenue
Bronx, NY 10463
(718) 548-0243

Clifford Wallach
(Folk Art)
81 Washington Street, #7J
Brooklyn, NY 11201
(718) 596-5325

Van Polla
(Movie Posters)
16-64 155 Street
Flushing, NY 11357-3233
(718) 746-0911

Mike Stakis
(Political Items)
3 Brookside Avenue, Room #3
Newburgh, NY 12550
(914) 568-0236

Joe De Gennaro
(Matchbook Covers)
309 East 87th Street, Apt. 6E
New York, NY 10128
(212) 975-4108

Robert Hess
(Sheet Music)
155 West 72nd Street, Suite 404
New York, NY 10023
(212) 579-0689

Stanley King
(Sheet Music)
260 Fifth Avenue
New York, NY 10001-6408
(212) 447-1880

Helaine Fendelman,
Helaine Fendelman & Associates
(Folk Art; Author of *Official Identification and Price Guide to American Folk Art*)
1248 Post Road
Scarsdale, NY 10583
(914) 725-0292

Kenneth Smith
(Military Collectibles)
55 Howard Avenue
Staten Island, NY 10301

Don Black
(Stamps)
405 Tarrytown Road, Suite 402
White Plains, NY 10607
(914) 347-3971

North Carolina

Fred Kahn
38 Dover Street
Asheville, NC 28804
(828) 252-6507 (Postcards)

Joseph Mashburn
(Postcards)
P.O. Box 609-M,
Enka, NC 28728
(828) 667-1427

Ohio

James Kesterson
(Stamps)
3881 Fulton Grove Road
Cincinnati, OH 45245
(513) 752-0949

Carl Albrecht
(Stamps)
P.O. Box 82252
Columbus, OH 43202
calbrech@infinet.com

Ivan Gilbert, M.D., Miran Art & Books
(Folk Art)
2824 Elm Avenue
Columbus, OH 42209
(614) 231-3707

Betty Powell
(Postcards)
P.O. Box 571
Columbus, OH 43085
(614) 885-1962

Marty Davis, Vintage Film Posters
(Movie Posters)
15875 Van Aken Boulevard, Suite 304C
Shaker Heights, OH 44120

John Williams
(Matchbook Covers)
1359 Surrey Road, Department CH
Vandalia, OH 45377-1646
(937) 890-8684

Oklahoma

Dale Peterson
(Advertising Items)
22762 Woodridge Drive
Claremore, OK 74017
(918) 341-5475

Ron Willis
(Military Collectibles)
2110 Fox Avenue
Moore, OK 73160
(580) 357-8000

Dean Hodgdon
(Matchbook Covers)
2920 East 77th Street
Tulsa, OK 74136-8723
(918) 494-0225

Ed Royse
(World War I and World War II
Recruiting Posters)
112 North Broadway Street
Walters, OK 73572
(580) 357-8000

Oregon

Tom Osjecki
(Stamps)
P.O. Box 792
Canyonville, OR 97417
(541) 839-4135

Marge Day
(Sheet Music)
17401 S.E. 39th Street
Portland, OR 98683
(360) 253-8233

John Gearhart
(Political Items)
3267 S.E. Hawthorne
Portland, OR 97214
(503) 255-8108

Margaret Horning
(Sheet Music)
13447 S.E. Brush Street
Portland, OR 97236-3323
(503) 761-3817

Jeanne Koch
(Sheet Music)
4312 S.E. Flavel Street
Portland, OR 97206
(503) 771-2024

Pennsylvania

Mike Landis
(Matchbook Covers)
P.O. Box 814
Adamstown, PA 19501
(888) 248-2291

Barry Hunsberger
(Advertising Items)
2300 Meadowlane Drive
Easton, PA 18042
(610) 253-2477

George Theofiles
(Movie Posters)
P.O. Box 1776
New Freedom, PA 17349-0076
(717) 235-4766

Dr. James Lewis Lowe
(Postcards)
P.O. Box 8
Norwood, PA 19074
(610) 485-8572

Marc Edelman
(Matchbook Covers)
8822 Hargrave Street
Philadelphia, PA 19152-1511
(215) 969-6258

Robert Kwalwasser
(Political Items)
168 Camp Fatima Road
Renfrew, PA 16053-9104
(724) 789-7766

Tennessee

Jon Warren
(Movie Posters)
P.O. Box 2512
Chattanooga, TN 37409
(423) 265-5515

Peggy Dillard
(Political Items)
P.O. Box 210904
Nashville, TN 37221-0904
(615) 646-1605

Texas

Gene Arnold
(Movie Posters)
2234 South Boulevard
Houston, TX 77098-5525
(713) 528-1880

Tony Zollo
(Stamps)
P.O. Box 150407
Lufkin, TX 75915-0407
zolloam@icc.net

Utah

Mario Donald Thomas
(Political Items, President
Harry S. Truman)
860 18th Avenue
Salt Lake City, UT 84103
(801) 532-5340

Vermont

Warren Rice
(Military Collectibles)
8 Orchard Terrace
Essex Junction, VT 05452-3501
(802) 878-3835

Virginia

Tom Morgan
(Sheet Music)
110 Monte Vista Avenue
Charlottesville, VA 22903-4117
(804) 296-9346

Gary Olsen
(Magazines, Postcards, Sheet Music)
505 South Royal Avenue
Front Royal, VA 22630
(540) 635-7157

John McClintock
(Postcards)
P.O. Box 1765
Manassas, VA 20108-1765
(703) 368-2757

Christopher B. Hearn
(Political Items)
125 Morven Park Road N.W.
Leesburg, VA 20176-2025
(703) 777-7181

Lewis Leigh Jr.
(Stamps)
38785 Leighfield Lane
Leesburg, VA 20175
(703) 771-3081

Bob Putnam
(Political Items)
9129 Lake Braddock Drive
Springfield, VA 22153
(703) 644-9711

Jon Radel
(Flags)
6917 Ridgeway Drive
Springfield, VA 22150-3027
jon@radel.com

Washington

Richard Lauck
(Matchbook Covers)
9424 Odin Way
Bothell, WA 98011-1164
(425) 486-4501

Dave Morris
(Postcards)
P.O. Box 1684
Port Orchard, WA 98366
(360) 871-7376

Ray L. Coughlin
(Stamps, Appraiser)
P.O. Box 762
Washougal, WA 98671
(360) 835-7990

Washington, DC

Ken Trombly
(Posters)
1050 17th Street N.W., Suite 1250
Washington, DC 20036
(800) 673-8158

Wisconsin

Mike Kranz
(Advertising Items)
463 Stage Line Road
Hudson, WI 54016-7849
(715) 386-7333

Foreign

Canada

Terry Stewart
71 John Street East
Waterloo, Ontario
N2J 1G2
Canada
(519) 745-1745

Clubs and Associations

*C*lubs and associations are one of the best sources for both the beginner and veteran collector. They offer a great opportunity to meet with other veteran collectors, learn and gather information, and have a good time. The clubs, organizations, and associations listed here reflect the latest information available at the time of publication and are subject to change. The list also represents an excellent cross section of the United States, Europe, and Asia-Pacific. Any active clubs, organizations, or associations that require a change of information or would like to be in the next edition of *American Patriotic Memorabilia* should send the required information to Michael Polak, P.O. Box 30328, Long Beach, CA 90853.

United States

Arizona

Remember That Song
(Sheet Music)
5623 North 64th Street
Glendale, AZ 85301

Tucson Post Card Exchange Club
820 Via Lucitas
Tucson, AZ 85718-1046
(520) 297-0980

California

Sierra-Diablo Matchcover Club/
Rathkamp Matchcover Society
12659 Echard Way
Auburn, CA 95603
rmseditor@ev1.net

American Society of Military History
1816 South Figueroa
Los Angeles, CA 90015
(213) 746-1776

National Sheet Music Society
1597 Fair Park Avenue
Los Angeles, CA 90041-2255

Angelus Matchcover Club
140 South Altadena Drive
Pasadena, CA 91104

San Francisco Bay Area Post Card Club
P.O. Box 621
Penngrove, CA 94951
(707) 795-2650

National Stamp Dealers Association
P.O. Box 7176
Redwood City, CA 94063
(800) 875-6633 or (650) 364-6667

San Diego Matchcover Club
161 North Meadowbrook Drive
San Diego, CA 92114
(619) 479-4505

Long Beach Matchcover Club
2501 West Sunflower, H-5
Santa Ana, CA 92704-7503
(714) 540-8220

Great War Society
P.O. Box 4585
Stanford, CA 94309
medwardh@hotmail.com

Hollywood Studio Collectors Club
(Movie Memorabilia)
3960 Laurel Canyon Boulevard, Suite 450
Studio City, CA 91604

International Stamp Collectors Society
P.O. Box 854
Van Nuys, CA 91408-0854
(818) 997-6496

Colorado

Tin Container Collectors Association
P.O. Box 440101
Aurora, CO 80044

Denver Strikers Matchcover Club
2630 South Garfield Way
Denver, CO 80210-5625

Trade Card Collector's Association
3706 South Acoma Street
Englewood, CO 80110

Connecticut

Connecticut Matchcover Club
197 Bradley Avenue
Hamden, CT 06514-3911

Company of Military Historians
North Main Street
Westbrook, CT 06498

Florida

Militaria Collectors Society of Florida
140 N.E. 55th Street
Fort Lauderdale, FL 33334
(954) 772-1420

CompuServe Stamp Chapter,
American Philatelic Society
2117 Greenway Drive
Winter Haven, FL 33881-1257
(941) 294-5279

Georgia

Atlanta Stamp Collectors Club
2442 King Point Drive
Atlanta, GA 30338-5927
(770) 986-4214

Hawaii

Hawai'i Postcard Club
P.O. Box 15273
Honolulu, HI 96830
(808) 922-2343

Nixon Collectors Organization
975 Maunawili Circle
Kailua, HI 96734

Illinois

Antique Advertising Association
of America
P.O. Box 1121
Morton Grove, IL 60053
adclub@pastimes.org

American Society of Artists
P.O. Box 1326
Palatine, IL 60078
(312) 751-2500

Advertising Cup and Mug Collectors
of America
P.O. Box 680
Solon, IL 52333

Windy City Matchcover Club
1307 College Avenue, Apt. 12
Wheaton, IL 60817
ltlb1t@aoal.com

Indiana

Indiana Political Collectors Club
P.O. Box 50022
Indianapolis, IN 46250-0022
(317) 845-1721

Indiana Stamp Club
P.O. Box 40792
Indianapolis, IN 46240
indypex@aol.com

Emerald City Club
(Movie Memorabilia)
153 East Main Street
New Albany, IN 47150

Kansas

Wichita Postcard Club
P.O. Box 780282
Wichita, KS 67278-0282
kskon@networksplus.net

Louisiana

Mid-South Matchcover Club
484 South 8th Street
Ponchatoula, LA 70454
(504) 386-2467

Maryland

Ford Political Items Collectors
18222 Flower Hill Way
Gaithersburg, MD 20879

Massachusetts

Sonneck Society for American Music
& Music in America
P.O. Box 476
Canton, MA 02021

Porcelain Advertising Collectors Club
P.O. Box 381
Marshfield Hills, MA 02051

Rainbow Study Unit of the American
Topical Association
(Stamps)
P.O. Box 632
Tewksbury, MA 01876-0632
(978) 851-8283

Minnesota

Angelus Matchcover Club
1231 Edmund Avenue
St. Paul, MN 55104
sjbnab@aol.com

Great Lakes Match Club
1000 Edgerton Street, #1313
St. Paul, MN 55101-3958
(651) 772-9398

Missouri

Gateway Postcard Club
P.O. Box 28941
St. Louis, MO 63132
jrpepper@inlink.com

Wolverine Matchcover Club
1984 South Western
Springfield, MO 65807

Montana

U.S. Philatelic Classics Society
P.O. Box 50127
Billings, MT 59105-0127
turgon96@aol.com

New Hampshire

Granite State Postcard Collectors Club
Rural Route #2, Box 3D, Parker Street
Canaan, NH 03741

New Jersey

South Jersey Postcard Club
11 South Lafayette Street
Cape May, NJ 08204-5301
(609) 884-3115

Orders and Medal Society of America
P.O. Box 484
Glassboro, NJ 08028

North American Vexillological
(Flag History) Association, PMB 225
1997 North Olden Avenue
Trenton, NJ 08618-2193
(207) 845-2857

United States Stamp Society
P.O. Box 722
Westfield, NJ 07091-0722
webmaster@usstamps.org

New Mexico

Folk Art Association of the Southwest
3993 Old Santa Fe Trail
Santa Fe, NM 87501
(505) 984-8680

New York

Fort Orange Stamp Club
128 Western Avenue
Altamont, NY 12009-6230
(518) 861-6256

Ephemera Society of America
(organization for collectors and dealers
of paper collectibles; Advertising)
P.O. Box 95
Cazenovia, NY 13035-0095
(315) 655-0139

Statue of Liberty Collectors Club
P.O. Box 535
Chautauqua, NY 14722

American Stamp Dealers Association
3 School Street, Suite 205
Glen Cove, NY 11542-2548
(516) 759-7000

New York Sheet Music Society
P.O. Box 354
Hewlett, NY 11557
(516) 295-0719

Empire Matchcover Club
481 Beacon Avenue
Lindenhurst, NY 11757

Casino Club
(Casino Matchcovers)
309 East 87th Street, #6E
New York, NY 10128

International Vintage Poster Dealers
Association
P.O. Box 501
New York, NY 10113-0501
(212) 355-8391

National Antiques & Art Dealers
Association of America
220 East 57th Street
New York, NY 10022
(212) 826-9707

Rail Splitter (Abraham Lincoln)
Box 275
New York, NY 10044

North Carolina

American Matchcover Collecting Club
P.O. Box 18481
Asheville, NC 28814-0481
(828) 254-4487

Western Film Preservation Society,
Raleigh Chapter
1012 Vance Street
Raleigh, NC 27608

Old Time Western Film Club
P.O. Box 142
Silver City, NC 27344

Ohio

American Philatelic Congress
P.O. Box 8171
Cincinnati, OH 45208
wandy001@aol.com

Girlie Matchcover Club
2583 Wexford Road
Columbus, OH 43221

Association of American Military
Uniform Collectors
P.O. Box 1876
Elyria, OH 44036

Civil War Collectors Society & The
American Militaria Exchange
5970 Taylor Ridge Drive
West Chester, OH 45069
(513) 874-0483

Oregon

Pacific Northwest Matchbook
Collectors Club
6225 S.W. Mad Hatter Lane
Beaverton, OR 97008

City of Roses Sheet Music
Collectors Club
17401 S.E. 39th Street
Portland, OR 98683
(360) 253-8233

Pennsylvania

Button Pushers
(Political Buttons)
P.O. Box 4
Coopersburg, PA 18036

National Association of Paper and
Advertising Collectibles
P.O. Box 500
Mount Joy, PA 17552

American Society of Military
Insignia Collectors
526 Lafayette Avenue
Palmerton, PA 18701

American Philatelic Society
P.O. Box 8000
State College, PA 16803-8000
(814) 237-3803

Liberty Bell Matchcover Club
2501 Maryland Avenue #7
Willow Grove, PA 19090-1835
billpjanp@msn.com

Texas

American Political Items Collectors
(APIC)
P.O. Box 1149
Adkins, TX 78101
(210) 945-2811

American Political Items Collectors
P.O. Box 340339
San Antonio, TX 78234

Washington

Pacific Northwest Matchcover
Collector's Club
9424 Odin Way
Bothell, WA 98011-1164
(425) 486-4501

Washington, DC

Big Boy Restaurants Club
(Big Boy Restaurants Matchcovers)
2713 Woodly Place N.W.
Washington, DC 20008

Virginia

American Association of
Philatelic Exhibitors
P.O. Box 1125
Falls Church, VA 22041-0125
jmhstamp@ix.netcom.com

Association of Professional Art Advisors
107 North Main Street
Farmville, VA 23901
(888) 682-2722

International Federation of Postcard
Dealers/Postcard History Society
P.O. Box 1765
Manassas, VA 20108
thewishbone@erols.com

Foreign

Australia

Australian Match Cover
Collectors Society
3 Milford Place
Bundorra, Victoria 3083
Australia

Sydney Phillumenist Club
(Matchcovers)
6 Rundle Street
Granville, NSW 2142
Australia

Austria

Susanne M. Meusel Vintage Postcards
Postfach 25
A-9586, 43-4257-4658
Austria

Belgium

Albert Denis
(Postcards)
121 rue des Hougnes
Verviers, B-4800
Belgium

Canada

British North American Philatelic
Society, Ltd.
5295 Moncton Street
Richmond, British Columbia V7E 3B2
Canada
(604) 272-5090

Quality Stamps & Covers
P.O. Box 296
St. Albert, Alberta T8N 1N3
Canada
(780) 460-2540

Southern Ontario Matchcover Club
44 Invermarge Drive
Scarborough, Ontario M1C 3M4
Canada
matches.tcmc@sympatico.ca

Trans-Canada Matchcover Club
151 Cooperage Cres.
Richmond Hill, Ontario L4C 9KA
Canada

England

British Film Institute
(History of Film and Movies)
21 Stephen Street
London WIP 2LN
U.K.
020-7255-1444

British Matchbox Label & Booklet
Society
122 High Street
Melbourn, Cambridgeshire SG8 6AL
U.K.
de9531@ida.utb.hb.se

Flag Institute
44 Middleton Road
Acomb, York, YO24 3AS
U.K.
44-1904-339985

Liverpool Philatelic Society, University of Liverpool
P.O. Box 147
Liverpool, L69 3BX
U.K.
44-151-794-5502

Medway and North Kent Phillumenist Club
(Matchcovers)
Brigadoon, the Street, Ulcombe, Maidstone, Kent ME17 1DX
U.K.

Postcard Traders Association, Glanrhyd Station House, Manordeilo, Llandeilo, Dyfed SA 19 7BP
U.K.
44-(0) 1550-777064

France

Assoc. Vitolphilique et Philumenique Francaise
(Matchcovers)
5 rue Ehrhardt 67300 Schiltigheim
France

Hong Kong

Chinese Phillumenic Society
(Matchcovers)
Box 60160
Tsat Tsz Mui P.O.
Hong Kong

Dealers

United States

Alabama

William Skelton, Highland's Vault
(Military/Historical Items)
P.O. Box 55448
Birmingham, AL 35255-5548
(205) 939-1178

Atisans
(American Folk Art)
P.O. Box 256
Mentone, AL 35984-0256
(256) 634-4037

Arizona

Terry and Norene Pavey
(Postcards)
P.O. Box 10614
Glendale, AZ 85318
(602) 439-2156

Fred Tenney
(Postcards)
6622 East Presidio Road
Scottsdale, AZ 85254
(480) 991-4566

Arkansas

Tom and Sara Mertens
(Postcards)
Carlisle, AR 72024
(501) 676-5493

Bill Burdick
(Postcards)
P.O. Box 441
Mountain Home, AR 72654
(870) 425-7799

California

Michael E. Johnson
(Postcards)
P.O. Box 3081
Alameda, CA 94501
(766) 724-5227

Heather Holmberg
(Movie Posters)
3727 West Magnolia Boulevard, #247
Burbank, CA 91505
(818) 765-7341

Heroes & Legends
(Movie Memorabilia)
P.O. Box 9088
Calabasas, CA 91372
(818) 346-9220

David J. DeLaurant
(Military Items)
1505 North Lafayette
Fresno, CA 93728
(559) 488-3229

Book City Collectibles
6631 Hollywood Boulevard
Hollywood, CA 90028
(323) 466-0120

Naomi Welch, Images of the Past
(author of *The Complete Works of*
Harrison Fisher, Illustrator and *American*
& European Postcards of Harrison Fisher,
Illustrator)
309 Playa Boulevard, Suite 110
La Selva Beach, CA 95076-1737
Fax: (831) 689-0318

Larry Edmunds, Larry Edmunds
BookShop
(Movie/Film Memorabilia)
6644 Hollywood Boulevard
Los Angeles, CA 90028-6208

Mike Rasmussen
(Postcards)
P.O. Box 726
Marina, CA 93933
(831) 759-0259

John and Nina Swanson
(Postcards)
26562 Guadiana
Mission Viejo, CA 92691
(949) 582-0905

Lynn Wenzel
(Sheet Music Collectibles)
15134 Airport Road
Nevada City, CA 95959
(530) 470-0360

Eddie Brandt's Saturday Matinee
(Movie Posters)
5006 Vineland Avenue
North Hollywood, CA 91601
(818) 506-4242

Mark Welch
(Movie Posters)
5820 Stoneridge Mall Road, Suite 100
P.O. Box 11355
Pleasanton, CA 94588
(925) 462-8483

James Dietz, J. S. Dietz Vintage
Movie Posters
(Movie Posters)
2726 Shelter Island Drive
San Diego, CA 92106
(619) 223-1563

Robert Richshafer
(Political/Historical Americana)
2929 First Avenue #L
San Diego, CA 92103
(619) 294-7950

William Rumpf, Memorabilia Mine
(Movie/Film Memorabilia)
P.O. Box 21026
San Jose, CA 95151
(408) 270-1072

Flag Store
20089 Broadway
Sonoma, CA 95476
(707) 996-8140

American Garage, Purveyors of
American Country & Folk Art
6545 Costello Avenue
Van Nuys, CA 91401
(818) 989-7474

Bick International
(Movie Memorabilia)
P.O. Box 854
Van Nuys, CA 91408
(818) 988-6496

Colorado

Randall Birnforf, Vintage Postcards
(Postcards)
1616 17th Street, Suite 268
Denver, CO 80202
(303) 628-5460

Charles J. Finley, Chuck Finley's
Postcards
(Postcards)
311 East Routt Avenue
Pueblo, CO 81004
(719) 543-0003

Connecticut

Jose L. and Aida S. Rodriguez and
Ove Braskerud
(Postcards)
430 Highland Avenue
P.O. Box 903
Cheshire, CT 06410

Andrew Levitt, Oldtime Stamp Shop
(Stamps)
P.O. Box 342
Danbury, CT 06813
(203) 743-5291

Martin Shapiro, Postcards International
(Postcards)
60-C Skiff Street, Suite 116
Handen, CT 06517
(203) 248-6621

Military Specialties
2543 Berlin Turnpike
Newington, CT 06111-4109
(860) 666-4275

Vaughn Mann, Cinema Recall
(Movie/Film Items)
P.O. Box 1021
New London, CT 06320
(840) 447-2286

Marguerite Riordan Antiques
(American Folk Art)
8 Pearl Street
Stonington, CT 06378
(860) 535-2511

University Archives
(Political/Historical Americana)
49 Richmondville Avenue
Westport, CT 06880
(800) 237-5692 or (203) 454-0111

William Guthman, Guthman Americana
(Military/Historical Items)
P.O. Box 392
Westport, CT 06881
(202) 259-9763

Delaware

Randy Gravenor, E.R.G. Militaria
(Military/Historical Items)
P.O. Box 299
Delmar, DE 19940
(410) 835-2280

Ernest C. Teichmann
(Postcards)
P.O. Box 403
Dover, DE 19903

Florida

Mildred D. Goheen
(Postcards)
6848 Tiburon Drive
Boca Raton, FL 33433
(561) 361-9201

Uncle Davey's Americana
(Political/Historical Americana)
6140 St. Augustine Road
Jacksonville, FL 32217
(904) 730-8932

Sandra Hollman, Global Music
Enterprises
(Sheet Music/Movie Memorabilia)
488 Archer Lane
Kissimmee, FL 34746
(407) 396-4176

Robert C. Blackburn
(Stamps and Postcards)
P.O. Box 1335
Lake Panasoffkee, FL 33538
(352) 793-9483

Ed Krohn
(Political Collectibles; author of
*National Political Convention Tickets
& Other Ephemera*)
P.O. Box 570699
Miami, FL 33257
(305) 237-2382

Robert Thames Art & Antiques
P.O. Box 4175
Ormond Beach, FL 32175
(904) 677-8835

Frank and Bill Muir, Grande Armee
Military Antiques, Via Gucci
(Military Collectibles)
256 Worth Avenue
Palm Beach, FL 33480
(800) 278-8212

Bengis Fine Art
1440 Coral Ridge Drive, #166
Pompano Beach, FL 33071
(954) 757-2444

Howard Hazelcorn
(Political Collectibles)
6731 Ashley Court
Sarasota, FL 34241-9696
(941) 921-1815

Sanders' Antique Mall
(American Folk Art)
22 North Lemon Avenue
Sarasota, FL 34236-5711
(941) 366-0400

Tom Peeling
(Political Items)
P.O. Box 6661
West Palm Beach, FL 33405-0661
(561) 585-1351

Georgia

Richard Moody
(Postcards)
1435 Peyton Place
Macon, GA 31211

Paul Kosek, P & K Military Antiques
(Military Collectibles)
1323 Washington Avenue
Savannah, GA 31401
(912) 355-6806

Idaho

Henry W. Taylor Jr.
500 South Main Street
P.O. Box 2247
Ketchum, ID 83340-2247
(208) 726-5757

Vernon W. Ham, Ham's Cards
(Postcards)
945 South 5th Street
St. Maries, ID 83861
(208) 245-4865

Illinois

Class Act Movie Posters
(Movie Posters)
2568 Stonehenge Drive
Aurora, IL 60504
(800) 380-6405 or (603) 499-8306

Roger Harvey, Card Source
(Postcards)
170 Selwyn Lane
Buffalo Grove, IL 60089-4333
(847) 520-8145

Joe Schulte
(Sheet Music Collectibles)
420 Wallace Street
Chicago Heights, IL 60411
(708) 877-7099

Charles G. Kratz, Jr.
(Military Items)
17821 Golfview
Homewood, IL 60430
(708) 799-8478

Darlene and Wally Schultz
(Postcards)
230 North Forest Court
Palatine, IL 60074
(847) 358-3226

Jim Mehrer, Jim Mehrer's Postal History
(Postcards/Stamps)
2405 30th Street
Rock Island, IL 61201
(309) 786-6539

Indiana

John W. Poling
(Military and Political Collectibles)
5998 South Ridgeview Road
Anderson, IN 46013-9774
(765) 778-2714

Michael McQuillen, Political Parade
Column-Antique Trader
(Political Collectibles)
P.O. Box 50022
Indianapolis, IN 46250-0022

Jerry Garrett, Jerry's Antiques & Postcards
(Postcards)
1807 West Madison Street
Kokomo, IN 46901-1829

Ted and Sallie Caldwell, Caldwell &
Company Civil War Antiques
(Military Collectibles, Revolutionary
War through Indian Wars)
816 Pleasant Street
Lebanon, IN 46052
(765) 482-0292

Al and Rhonda Hunter, Hunter's Vault
(Political Collectibles)
P.O. Box 720
Westfield, IN 46074-0720
(317) 815-1975

Iowa

Main Street Antiques & Art
(American Folk Art)
110 West Main
P.O. Box 340
West Branch, IA 52358-0340
(319) 643-2065

Ron Playle
(Postcards)
P.O. Box 65918
West Des Moines, IA 50265
(515) 279-0884

Kansas

Lonny L. Bauer
(Postcards)
730 East D. Avenue
Kingman, KS 67068

Hal N. Ottaway
(Postcards)
P.O. Box 780282
Wichita, KS 67278
(316) 686-5574

Kentucky

Roger S. Steffen, Steffen's Historical
Militaria
(Military Collectibles)
14 Murnan Road
Cold Spring, KY 41076
(859) 431-4499

Maine

Jon Allan, Elmer's Nostalgia
(Political Items)
3 Putnam Street
Sanford, ME 04073-2024
(207) 324-2166

Gary Guyette Antiques
(American Folk Art)
P.O. Box 522
West Farmington, ME 04992
(207) 778-6256

Maryland

Sheldon Dobres
(Postcards)
P.O. Box 1855
Baltimore, MD 21203-1855
(410) 486-6569

Larry L. King, Americana Resources
(Political Items)
18222 Flower Hill Way, #299
Gaithersburg, MD 20879-5300

Roy Cox
(author of *How to Price and Sell Old
Picture Postcards)*
P.O. Box 3610
Hamilton, MD 21214

Erik Padison, ISA
(Military Collectibles)
15127 Frederick Road
Rockville, MD 20850
(301) 424-0053

Cinderella Company
(Matchbook Covers)
P.O. Box 265
Sykesville, MD 21748-0265
(410) 549-2412

Massachusetts

Nancy Steinbock, Nancy Steinbock
Posters & Prints
12 Garrison Street
Chestnut, MA 02467
(800) 438-1577

John Clement
(Stamp Collecting)
36 Oakwood Avenue
Fitchburg, MA 01420-7421
(978) 345-5863

Rex Stark Americana
(Political/Historical Americana)
P.O. Box 1029
Gardner, MA 01440-6029
(978) 630-3237

Paul Longo, Paul Longo Americana
(Political Items)
P.O. Box 5510
Gloucester, MA 01930-0007
(978) 525-2290

Blue Cape Antiques
(Military Collectibles)
620 Great Road, Route 119
Littleton, MA 01460
(978) 486-4709

Susan Stella Antiques
(American Folk Art)
9 Masconomo Street
Manchester, MA 01944
(978) 526-7371

Richard Champagne
(Stamp Collectibles)
P.O. Box 600372
Newtonville, MA 02460-0004
(617) 969-5719

Siegfried Feller, Cartomania Plus
(Postcards)
8 Amherst Road
Pelham, MA 01002-9739
(413) 253-3115

Minnesota

Gerald E. Czulewicz, Sr., Antiques
Americana
(Uncle Sam Collectibles; author of
Foremost Guide to Uncle Sam Collectibles)
25699 Highway 65 N.E.
Isanti, MN 55040
(763) 444-9216

Bob Johnson
(Military Collectibles)
3915 Highway 7
Minneapolis, MN 55416
(952) 920-3820

Pat Olson
(Military Items)
4533 Rutledge Avenue
Minneapolis, MN 55436
(952) 927-0560

Bruce Hubbard IV, The Williams
Collection
(Movie/Film Memorabilia)
260 Ridgeview Drive
Wayzata, MN 55391
(612) 473-9591

Missouri

Sam Withers
(Paper Americana)
P.O. Box 19916
St. Louis, MO 63144
(314) 968-1647

Silver Screen Film Collectibles
(Movie Memorabilia)
6336 Clayton Avenue
St. Louis, MO 63139
(314) 781-0077

Bruce Hershenson, Hershenson-Allen
Archive
(Movie Posters)
P.O. Box 874
West Plains, MO 65775-0874
(417) 256-9616

Montana

Hayes Otoupalik
(Military Collectibles)
14000 Highway 93 North
Missoula, MT 59802
(406) 549-4817

Nevada

Gary L. Cohen, Political Memorabilia
Marketplace
(Political Collectibles)
10780 Elk Lake Drive
Las Vegas, NV 89144
(702) 233-0123

New Hampshire

Brookman/Barrett & Worthen
(Stamps)
10 Chestnut Drive
Bedford, NH 03110
(800) 332-3383

Beverly A. Hammer,
Beverly A. Hammer Sheet Music Sales
(Sheet Music Collectibles)
P.O. Box 75
East Derry, NH 03041
(603) 432-3528

Wayland Bunnell, Cleen Sheets
(Sheet Music Collectibles)
199 Tarrytown Road
Manchester, NH 03103-2723
(603) 668-5466

Richard Friz, Maddie's Muse
(Political Collectibles; author of
*The Official Price Guide to Political
Memorabilia*)
P.O. Box 472
Peterborough, NH 03458-0472
(603) 563-8155

RJG Antiques
(American Folk Art)
P.O. Box 60
Rye, NH 03870
(603) 433-1770

David Bowers, Bowers & Merena, Inc.
(American Film Posters)
P.O. Box 1224
Wolfeboro, NH 03894-1224
(800) 458-4646 or (603) 569-5095

New Jersey

Susan and Mario Carrandi,
Carrandi Vintage Posters
122 Monroe Avenue
Belle Mead, NJ 08502-4608
(908) 874-0630

Alan Levine
(American Film Posters)
P.O. Box 1577
Bloomfield, NJ 07003
(973) 743-5288

George Dembo
(Posters)
P.O. Box 657
Chatham, NJ 07928 0657
(973) 701-0713

Cobweb Collectibles & Ephemera
(Sheet Music, Postcards)
9 Walnut Avenue
Cranford, NJ 08016

Sandy Marrone
(Sheet Music Collectibles)
113 Oakwood Drive
Cinnaminson, NJ 08077
(856) 829-6104

Poster World
(Movie Posters)
9 Bolton Place
Fair Lawn, NJ 07410
(201) 791-1073

David Grimes
(Posters, Advertising)
P.O. Box 354
Hopewell, NJ 08525
(609) 466-0303

New Mexico

George Baxley
(Stamp Collectibles)
P.O. Box 807
Alamogordo, NM 88311
(505) 437-8707

Richard Frajola
(Stamp Collectibles)
P.O. Box 2679
Ranchos De Taos, NM 87557
(501) 751-7607

Louis Bixeman, International Vintage
Poster Fair
36 Vereda Serena
Santa Fe, NM 87505-5918
(800) 856-8069

New York

Golden Philatelics, Jack and Myrna
Golden
P.O. Box 484
Cedarhurst, NY 11516
(516) 791-1804

Muleskinner Antiques
(American Folk Art)
10626 Main Street
Clarence, NY 14031
(716) 759-2661

John Kisch, Separate Cinema Archive
P.O. Box 114
Hyde Park, NY 12438-0114
(845) 452-1998

Doris Bode, Passport Stamps Company
(Stamps)
P.O. Box 637
Lynbrook, NY 11563
(516) 295-3643

American Coin & Stamp Brokerage
30 Merrick Avenue
Merrick, NY 11566
(516) 546-2300

Henry Gitner, Henry Gitner Philatelists
2020 Low Avenue, Suite 311
P.O. Box 3077
Middletown, NY 10940
(800) 947-8267

Harvey and Sandy Dolin,
Harvey Dolin & Company
(Stamp Collectibles)
111 Fulton Street, Mezzanine Level
New York, NY 10386
(212) 267-0216

Hirsch & Adler Galleries
21 East 70th Street
New York, NY 10021
(212) 535-8810

Peter Hlinka Historical Americana
(Political/Historical Americana)
P.O. Box 310
New York, NY 10028-0017
(718) 409-6407

Sam Malamud, Ideal Stamp Company
(Stamp Collectibles)
460 West 34th Street
New York, NY 10001
(212) 629-7979

J. R. Stamps, John Rerecic
30 West 26th Street
New York, NY 10001
(212) 663-4134 or (212) 807-6477

Joe Burtis, Motion Picture Arts Gallery
133 East 58th Street, 10th Floor
New York, NY 10022
(212) 223-1009

Jerry Ohlinger's Movie Material Store
(Movie Posters)
242 West 14th Street
New York, NY 10011-7206
(212) 989-0869

Max Davis, Postcards of the World
New York Antique Center
(Postcards)
26 West 25th Street, Shop #10
New York, NY 10010
(212) 243-7090

Sam Sarowitz, Posteritati Movie Posters
(Movie Posters)
241 Centre Street, Suite 5F
New York, NY 10013-3224
(212) 226-2207

Kenneth W. Rendell Gallery
(Political/Historical Americana)
989 Madison Avenue
New York, NY 10021
(800) 447-1007 or (212) 717-1776

Ricco/Maresca Gallery
(American Folk Art)
529 West 20th Street, Third Floor
New York, NY 10011
(212) 627-4819

Sholl Antiques
(American Folk Art)
P.O. Box 9
Norwood, NY 13668
(315) 353-2474

Sheet Music Center
(Sheet Music Collectibles)
Box 10
Old Bethpage, NY 11804
(800) 527-7626

Todd Richard Feiertag, Poster City
(Movie Posters)
P.O. Box 94
Orangeburg, NY 10962-0094
(800) 272-3323 or (201) 869-1692

Eric Kane
(Military/Historical Items)
285 Sills Road, Building #7
Patchogue, NY 11772
(516) 475-2144

Debra Clifford, Vintage Poster Works
(Posters)
P.O. Box 88
Pittsford, NY 14534
(716) 218-9483

Helaine Fendelman & Associates
(author of *The Official Identification and
Price Guide to American Folk Art*)
1248 Post Road
Scarsdale, NY 10583-2153
(914) 725-0292

Harry Hagendorf, Columbian Stamp
Company
(Stamp Collectibles)
700 White Plains Road
Scarsdale, NY 10583
(914) 725-2290

Jacques Noel Jacobsen, Jr.
Collector's Antiquities
(Military/Historical Items)
60 Manor Road
Staten Island, NY 10310-2698
(718) 981-0973

Raymond J. Zyla
(Military Collectibles)
P.O. Box 399
Utica, NY 13503-0399
(315) 893-7888

North Carolina

Bill Reskin
(author of *The Matchcover Resource Book
and Price Guide*)
P.O. Box 18481
Asheville, NC 28814-0481
(828) 254-4487

Animation & Fine Art Galleries
200 North Greensboro Street,
Car Mill Mall
Carrboro, NC 27510
(919) 968-8008

Joseph L. Mashburn, Colonial House
(Postcards; publisher of *The Postcard
Price Guide, The Artist-Signed Postcard
Price Guide,* and *Super Rare Postcards of
Harrison Fisher*)
P.O. Box 609-M
Enka, NC 28728-0609
(828) 667-1427

Seaside Art Gallery
P.O. Box 1
2716 Virginia Dare Trail South
Nags Head, NC 27959
(252) 441-5418

Newton Carter
(Military Collectibles)
P.O. Box 46
Wallace, NC 28466
(910) 285-5506

Ohio

Tregoning Fine Art & Services
100 North Main Street
Chagrin Falls, OH 44022
(440) 247-1690

Jeannie Peters, Mt. Washington Antiques
(Sheet Music Collectibles)
3742 Kellogg Avenue
Cincinnati, OH 45226-1514

Oregon

Tom Osjecki
(Postcards/Stamps)
P.O. Box 792
Cayonville, OR 97417
(541) 839-4135

Lewis & Bond Fine Art
209 West Houghton Street
Medford, OR 97501
(541) 988-5484

Pennsylvania

Ken Kipp, Allenwood Americana
Antiques
(Military/Historical Items)
P.O. Box 116
Allenwood, PA 17810-0016
(570) 538-1440

Heritage Collectors' Society
(Political/Historical Americana)
P.O. Box 2131
Doylestown, PA 18901
(215) 230-9421

J. T. Gallaghan, Faded Glories
(Military Collectibles)
Drexel Hill, PA 19026
(215) 370-6138

Dale Enterprises
P.O. Box 539
Emmaus, PA 18049
(610) 433-3303

Dale and Debra Anderson
(Military/Historical Items)
4 West Confederate Avenue
Gettysburg, PA 17325
(717) 334-1031

James M. Russell
(Political Items)
7 Meadow Lane
Gettysburg, PA 17325-8025
(717) 337-9018

Terry Hannon, President,
Phoenix Militaria
(Military Collectibles)
P.O. Box 245
Lyon Station, PA 19536
(610) 682-1010

George Theofiles
(Movie Posters/Advertising)
P.O. Box 1776
New Freedom, PA 17349-0076
(717) 235-4766

Bob and Kay Schies
(Postcards)
452 East Bissell Avenue
Oil City, PA 16301-2063
(814) 677-3182

Bill Fisher
(Movie Posters)
16104 Delaire Landing Road
Philadelphia, PA 19114
(888) 3-POSTER

Jay Miller
(Postcards)
725 South Schell Street
Philadelphia, PA 19147
(215) 925-3839

Barbara's Stars
(Movie Memorabilia)
P.O. Box 723
Smethport, PA 16749
(814) 887-5110

Timothy Hughes, Rare & Early
Newspapers
(Patriotic Newspapers: *Colonial,
Harper's Weekly,* Civil War titles)
P.O. Box 3636
Williamsport, PA 17701

Michael Burke, Kats Militaria
(Military/Historical Americana)
P.O. Box 20519
York, PA 17402
(717) 699-4448

Rhode Island

George Van Duinwyk, Articles of War
(Military/Historical Items)
358 Boulevard
Middletown, RI 02842
(401) 846-8503

Frank C. Perreault
(Postcards)
239 Pierce Avenue
Warwick, RI 02888
(401) 781-7474

Tom & Dave's Militaria
(Military Collectibles)
P.O. Box 725
Wyoming, RI 02898

South Carolina

Andrew Lipps, Wartime Collectables
(Military/Historical Items)
P.O. Box 165
539 Dekalb Street
Camden, SC 29020
(803) 424-5273

Scott Vezeau
(Military Collectibles)
P.O. Box 10400
Columbia, SC 29207
(803) 865-8868

America Oh Yes!
(American Folk Art)
P.O. Box 3075
Hilton Head Island, SC 29938
(843) 785-2649

Big Sky Enterprises
(Military and Historical Indian
Collectibles)
P.O. Box 493
Piedmont, SC 29673
(864) 299-1375

Tennessee

Cinemode
(Movie Posters)
138 Second Avenue North, Suite #104
Nashville, TN 37201
(615) 742-3048

Texas

Drew Julian, Drew Julian's Political
Collectibles
(Political Collectibles)
P.O. Box 150363
Austin, TX 78715-0363
(512) 447-8785

Ronald E. Wade
(Political Collectibles)
2100 Lafayette Drive
Longview, TX 75601-3417
(903) 236-9615

Utah

Warren Anderson, America West
Archives
(Military/Historical Items)
P.O. Box 100
Cedar City, UT 84721-7323
(435) 586-9497

Vermont

Jim and Kayce Dimond
(Postcards)
P.O. Box 362
Pittsford, VT 05763
(802) 483-6610

Virginia

R. Neil Reynolds, Fine Old Posters
(Posters)
1015 King Street
Alexandria, VA 22314-2922
(703) 684-3656

LTC (Ret) Thomas M. Johnson,
Reference Books & Militaria
(Military Collectibles)
403 Chataham Square Office Park
Fredericksburg, VA 22405
(540) 373-9150

Ernie White
(Postcards)
Box 28766
Richmond, VA 20108
(804) 262-5230

Richard Fleming
(Military Items)
P.O. Box 8394
Virginia Beach, VA 23450
(757) 622-1343

Washington

Ruth A. Miller Knott
(Political Items)
2601 Kittias Highway
Ellensburg, WA 98926
(509) 962-8840

Charles Zeder, Zeder's Antiques
(Political Items)
1320 S.W. 10th Street
North Bend, WA 98045
(425) 888-6697

Robert Candel, Movie Poster Shop
(Movie Posters)
1314 South Grand Boulevard, #2-156
Spokane, WA 99202
(403) 250-7588

West Virginia

Stephen Cresswell
(Political Items)
Route 1, Box 185-A
Buckhannon, WV 26201
cress@msys.net

Curtis and Ruth Duckett
(Postcards)
P.O. Box 674 M
Rainelle, WV 25962
(304) 438-7659

Wisconsin

Last Square
(Military Collectibles)
5944 Odana Road
Madison, WI 53719
(800) 750-4401

Foreign
Canada

Wray Martin
(Matchbook Covers)
221 Upper Paradise
Hamilton, Ontario L9C 5C1
Canada
(905) 383-0454

Thomas Bauer, Nonstop Collectibles
(Movie/Film Memorabilia)
6152 Terrebonne
Montreal, Quebec H4B 1A3
Canada
(514) 489-5499

Dave Rassay
(Stamp Collectibles)
5900 Explorer Drive
Mississauga, Ontario L4W 5L2
Canada
(905) 361-4189

England

Dauwaladers of Salisbury
(Stamp Collectibles)
92/96 Fisherton Street
Salisbury SP2 7QY
U.K.
01722-412100

Eric Lilley
(Movie/Film Memorabilia)
Charles Clore Court, Flat 59
139 Appleford Road
Reading Berkshire RG30 3NT
U.K.
01635-869694

France

Maurice and Laya Jakubowicz,
Affiche Francaise
(Posters)
128 Avenue do la Chevre d'Or
Bazincourt/Epte, 06220
France
(33) 0-493-63-45-92

Germany

Walter Christ
(Stamp Collectibles)
Gutwerkstr. 30
Aschaffenburg, 63743
Germany
0049-6021-98407

Museum and Research Resources

United States

Arizona

Postal History Foundation
P.O. Box 40725
Tucson, AZ 85717
(520) 623-6652

California

American Film Institute
2021 North Western Avenue
Los Angeles, CA 90027
(323) 856-7600

Archives of American Art,
West Coast Research Center,
Huntington Library
1151 Oxford Road
San Marino, CA 91108
(626) 583-7847

Friends of the Western Philatelic Library
P.O. Box 2219
Sunnyvale, CA 94087
(408) 733-0336

Getty Center
1200 Getty Center Drive
Los Angeles, CA 90049
(310) 440-7300

Military Antiques & Museum
300 Petaluma Boulevard North
Petaluma, CA 94942
(707) 763-2220

San Diego County Philatelic Library
7403 C. Princess View Drive
San Diego, CA 92120
(619) 229-8813

Western Philatelic Library
P.O. Box 2219
Sunnyvale, CA 94087
(408) 733-0336

Connecticut

Museum of American Political Life,
University of Hartford
200 Bloomfield Avenue
West Hartford, CT 06117
(860) 768-4090

Georgia

High Museum of Art
1280 Peachtree Street
Atlanta, GA 30309
(404) 733-4400

Illinois

Lake County Discovery Museum,
Curt Teich Postcards Archives
27277 Forest Preserve Drive
Wauconda, IL 60084-2016
(847) 968-3381

Los Angeles County Museum of Art
5905 Wilshire Boulevard
Los Angeles, CA 90036
(323) 857-6000

Spencer Weisz Galleries
(Vintage Posters)
214 West Ohio Street
Chicago, IL 60610
(312) 527-9420

Maryland

Walters Art Museum
600 North Charles Street
Baltimore, MD 21201
(410) 547-9000

Massachusetts

American Antiquarian Society
185 Salisbury Street
Worcester, MA 01609
(508) 755-5221

Boston Museum of Fine Arts
465 Huntington Avenue
Boston, MA 02115
(617) 267-9300

Spellman Museum of Stamps and
Postal History
235 Wellesley Street
Weston, MA 02193
(781) 768-8367

Michigan

Detroit Institute of Art
5300 Woodward Avenue
Detroit, MI 48202
(313) 833-7900

New Jersey

Newark Museum of Art
49 Washington Street
P.O. Box 540
Newark, NJ 07101-0540
(973) 596-6550

New Mexico

Museum of International Folk Art
706 Camino Lejo
P.O. Box 2065
Santa Fe, NM 87505-2065

New York

Albany Institute of History & Art
125 Washington Avenue
Albany, NY 12210
(518) 463-4478

American Museum of the Moving Image
35th Avenue at 36th Street
Astoria, NY 11106
(718) 784-4520

Archives of American Art,
New York Research Center
1285 Avenue of the Americas
New York, NY 10019
(212) 399-5015

Chisholm Larsson Gallery
(Vintage Posters)
145 Eighth Avenue
New York, NY 10011
(212) 741-1703

Collectors Club Research Library
(Philatelic)
22 East 35th Street
New York, NY 10016-3806
(212) 683-0559

Library & Museum of
the Performing Arts
40 Lincoln Center Plaza
New York, NY 10023-7498
(212) 870-1630

Metropolitan Museum of Art
1000 Fifth Avenue
New York, NY 10028-0198
(212) 535-7710

Museum of American Folk Art
Columbus Avenue at 66th Street
New York, NY 10023-6214
(212) 977-7298

Park South Gallery at Carnegie Hall
(Rare Posters)
154 West 57th Street, Studio 11-114
New York, NY 10019
(212) 246-5900

Ohio

Cleveland Museum of Art
11150 East Boulevard
Cleveland, OH 44106-1797
(216) 421-7340

Toledo Museum of Art
2445 Monroe Street
Toledo, OH 43697
(419) 255-8000

Oregon

American Advertising Museum
211 N.W. Fifth Avenue and Davis Street
Portland, OR 97209
(503) 226-0000

Pennsylvania

American Philatelic Research Library
P.O. Box 8000
State College, PA 16803-8000
(814) 237-3803

Pennsylvania Academy of Fine Arts
118 North Broad Street
Philadelphia, PA 19102
(215) 972-7600

Philadelphia Museum of Art
P.O. Box 7646
Philadelphia, PA 10101-7646
(215) 684-7860

Texas

Wineburgh Philatelic Research Library,
University of Texas at Dallas
P.O. Box 830643
Richardson, TX 75083-0643
(972) 883-2570

Virginia

Abby Aldrich Rockefeller
Folk Art Center
P.O. Box 1776
Williamsburg, VA 23187-1776
(757) 229-1000

Washington, D.C.

Daughters of the American
Revolution Museum
1776 D Street N.W.
Washington, DC 20006-5392
(202) 879-3241

Library of Congress American
Folklife Center
101 Independence Avenue S.E.
Washington, DC 20540-4610
(202) 707-5510

National Museum of American History,
Archives Center, Smithsonian Institution
14th and Constitution Avenue N.W.
Washington, DC 20560
(202) 357-3270

National Postal Museum
2 Massachusetts Avenue N.E.
Washington, DC 20560-0001
(202) 633-9360

Naval Historical Center,
Washington Navy Yard
805 Kidder Breese S.E.
Washington, DC 20374-5060
(202) 433-4882

U.S. Marine Corps Historical Center &
Museum, Washington Navy Yard,
Building 58
1254 Charles Morris Street S.E.
Washington, DC 20374-0540
(202) 433-3483

Auction Houses and Services

AAG, International Militaria Mail
Auction
1226-B Sans Souci Parkway
Wilkes Barre, PA
(570) 822-5300

Donald Ackerman
(Historical Items)
P.O. Box 3487
Wallington, NJ 07057
(973) 779-8785

Albert Post Galleries
809 Lucerne Avenue
Lake Worth, FL 33460
(561) 582-4477

Albrecht & Cooper Auction Services
3884 Saginaw Road
Vassar, MI 48768
(517) 823-8835

Sanford Alderfer Auction Company
501 Fairgrounds Road
Hatfield, PA 19440
(215) 393-3000,
www.alderfer-company.com

Anderson Auction, Al Anderson
(Political Items)
P.O. Box 644
Troy, OII 45373-0644
(937) 339-0850

Antique Pottery/Stoneware Auctions,
Bruce and Vicki Waasdorp
P.O. Box 434
Clarence, NY 14031
(716) 759-2361, Fax: 759-2379,
waasdorp@antiques-stoneware.com,
www.antiques-stoneware.com

Apple Tree Auction Center
1616 West Church Street
Newark, OH 43055
(614) 344-4282

Armans of Newport
207 High Point Avenue
Portsmouth, RI 02871

Arthur Auctioneering, RD 2
P.O. Box 155
Hughesville, PA 17737
(717) 584-3697

Autopia Advertising Auctions
19937 N.E. 154th Street, Building C2
Woodinville, WA 98072
(425) 883-7653

Noel Barrett Antiques & Auctions, Ltd.
P.O. Box 1001
Carversville, PA 18913
(610) 297-5109

Beck Auctions, Dave Beck
(Advertising)
P.O. Box 435
Mediapolis, IA 52637-0435
(319) 394-3943

Bel-Aire Stamp Auctions
(Stamps)
2589 Hamline Avenue, North, Suite D
St. Paul, MN 55113
(612) 633-8533

Bill Bertoia Auctions
1881 Spring Road
Vineland, NJ 08360
(609) 692-1881

Beverly Hills Auctioneers
9454 Wilshire Boulevard, Suite 202
Beverly Hills, CA 90212
(310) 278-8115

Bidders Antiques
241 South Union Street
Lawrence, MA 01843
(508) 688-4347

Boos Gallery, Frank Boos
420 Enterprise Court
Bloomfield Hills, MI 48302
(248) 332-1500

Bothroyd & Detwiler Online Auctions
1290 8th Avenue
Yuma, AZ
detwiler@primenet.com
www.primenet.com/~detwiler/index.html

Brown Auctions
900 East Kansas
Greensburg, KS 67054
(316) 723-2111

Buffalo Bay Auction Company
5244 Quam Circle
Rogers, MN 55374
(612) 428-8440
www.buffalobayauction.com

Butterfield, Butterfield & Dunning
755 Church Road
Elgin, IL 60123
(847) 741-3483
www.butterfields.com

Butterfields
220 San Bruno Avenue
San Francisco, CA 94103
(415) 861-7500
www.butterfields.com

C. C. Auction Gallery
416 Court
Clay Center, KS 67432
(913) 632-6021

W. E. Channing & Company
53 Old Santa Fe Trail
Santa Fe, NM 87501
(505) 988-1078

Chicago Art Galleries
5039 Oakton Street
Skokie, IL 60077
(847) 677-6080

Christie's
502 Park Avenue
New York, NY 10022
(212) 546-1000
www.christies.com

Christie's
(Art/Antiques)
20 Rockefeller Plaza
New York, NY 10020
(212) 636-2000

Cincinnati Art Galleries
635 Main Street
Cincinnati, OH 45202
(513) 381-2128

Cohasco, Inc., Robert Snyder
(Historical Items)
P.O. Box 821
Yonkers, NY 10702-0821
(914) 476-8500

Collection Liquidators Auction Service
341 Lafayette Street
New York, NY 10012
(212) 505-2455
www.rtam.com/coliq/bid.html

Collectors Auction Services
Route 2, Box 431, Oakwood Drive
Oil City, PA 16301
(814) 677-6070

Collectors Sales & Services
P.O. Box 4037
Middletown, RI 02842
(401) 849-5012
collectors@antiquechina.com
www.antiqueglass.com/homepage.htm

Cokepe Auction
226 Route 7A
Cokepe, NY 12516
(518) 329-1142

Cowan's Auctions, C. Wesley Cowan
(Historical Items)
747 Park Avenue
Terrace Park, OH 45174
(513) 248-8122

Craftsman Auction
1485 West Housatoric
Pittsfield MA, 01202
(413) 442-7003
www.artsncrafts.com

Dargate Auction Galleries
5607 Baum Boulevard
Pittsburgh, PA 15206
(412) 362-3558
www.dargate.com

Down-Jersey Auction
15 Southwest Lakeside Drive
Medford, NJ 08055
(609) 953-1755, Fax: 609-953-5351
dja@skyhigh.com
www.down-jersey.com

William Doyle Galleries
175 East 87th Street
New York, NY 10128-2205
(212) 427-2730
www.doylegalleries.com

Dunbar Gallery
76 Haven Street
Milford, MA 01757
(508) 634-8697

Early American History Auction
P.O. Box 3341
La Jolla, CA 92038
(858) 459-4159

Early Auction Company
123 Main Street
Milford, OH 45150
(513) 831-4833

East Coast Books
(Historical Items)
P.O. Box 849
Wells, ME 04090
(207) 646-3584

Steve Finer Rare Books
P.O. Box 758
Greenfield, MA 01302
(413) 773-5811

Charles G. Firby Auctions
6695 Highland Road, Suite 107
Waterford, MI 48327
(248) 666-5333

Freeman/Fine Arts Company of
Philadelphia
1808 Chestnut Street
Philadelphia, PA 19103
(215) 563-9275

Gallery at Knotty Pine Auction Service
Route 10, P.O. Box 96
West Swanzey, NH 03469
(603) 352-2313, Fax: (603) 352-5019
kpa@inc-net.com
www.knottypineantiques.com

Garth's Auctions
2690 Stratford Road
Box 369
Delaware, OH 43015
(740) 362-4771, Fax: (740) 363-0164
info@garths.com, www.garths.com

Glass Works Auctions
Box 187
East Greenville, PA 18041
(215) 679-5849, Fax: (215) 679-3068
glswrk@enter.net
www.glswrk-auction.com

Gore Enterprises, William D. Emberley
P.O. Box 158
Huntington, VT 05462
(802) 453-3311

Grogan & Company Auctioneers,
Michael B. Grogan
(Art)
22 Harris Street
Dedham, MA 02026
(781) 461-9500

Hake's Americana & Collectibles
Auction, Ted Hake
(Historical Items)
P.O. Box 1444
York, PA 17405-1444
(717) 848-1333

Hamer Rooke Galleries
32 East 57th Street
New York, NY 10022
(212) 751-1900

Hammer Sheet Music Sales,
Beverly A. Hammer
(Sheet Music)
P.O. Box 75
East Derry, NH 03041
(603) 432-3528

Gene Harris Antique Auction Center
203 South 18th Avenue
P.O. Box 476
Marshalltown, IA 50158
(515) 752-0600
www.harrisantiqueauction.com

Harris Auctions, U. I. "Chick" Harris
(Historical Items)
1010 Lemon Street
Highland, IL 62249-1678
(618) 651-1144

Norman C. Heckler & Company
79 Bradford Corner Road
Woodstock Valley, CT 06282
(860) 974-1634, Fax: (860) 974-2003
heckler@neca.com
www.hecklerauction.com

Willis Henry Auctions, Willis Henry
(Folk Art/Art/Antiques)
22 Main Street
Marshfield, MA 02050
(781) 834-7774

James E. Hill Auctions
P.O. Box 366
Randolph, VT 05060
(802) 728-5465
jehantqs@sover.net

Historical Collectible Auctions,
Robert Raynor
P.O. Box 975
Burlington, NC 27215
(336) 570-2803

Historicana, Robert Coup
(Political Items)
P.O. Box 348
Leola, PA 17540-0348
(717) 656-7855

Randy Inman Auctions
(Advertising)
P.O. Box 726
West Buxton, ME 04093
(207) 872-6900

James D. Julia Auctioneers
(Advertising)
Route 201, Skowhegan Road
P.O. Box 830
Fairfield, ME 04937
(207) 453-7125

Daniel F. Kelleher Company
Stanley J. Richmond
(Stamps)
24 Farnsworth Street, Suite 605
Boston, MA 02210-1264
(617) 443-0033

Manion's Auction House
P.O. Box 12214
Kansas City, KS 66112
(913) 299-6692

Greg Manning Auctions, Greg Manning
(Stamps)
775 Passaic Avenue
West Caldwell, NJ 07006
(973) 882-0004

Mapes Auctioneering & Appraisers
1729 Vestal Parkway
Vestal, NY 13850
(607) 754-9193

McMurray Antiques & Auctions
P.O. Box 393
Kirkwood, NY 13795
Phone/Fax: (607) 775-2321

Militaria Collectibles Auction Haus,
Gilbert Shatto
(Military Collectibles)
900 Hilton Drive
Fayetteville, NC 28311-2540

Mohawk Arms, Raymond J. Zyla
P.O. Box 399
Utica, NY 13503
(315) 893-7888

Wm. Morford
Rural Route #2
Cazenovia, NY 13035
(315) 662-7625, Fax: (315) 662-3570
norf2bid@aol.com
www.morfauction.com

Muddy River Trading Company,
Gary Metz
P.O. Box 18185
Roanoke, VA 24014
(540) 982-3886

Neal Auction Company
4038 Magazine Street
New Orleans, LA 70115
(504) 899-5329
nealauction.com

New England Absentee Auctions
16 Sixth Street
Stamford, CT 06905
(203) 975-9055, Fax: (203) 323-6407
neaauction@aol.com

New England Auction Gallery
P.O. Box 2273
West Peabody, MA 01960
(508) 535-3140

Nostalgia Publications
21 South Lake Drive
Hackensack, NJ 07601
(201) 488-4536
www.nosstalgiapubls.com

Richard Opfer Auctioneering
1919 Greenspring Drive
Timonium, MD 21093
(410) 252-5035
www.opferauction.com

Don Osborne Auctions
33 Eagleville Road
Orange, MA 01354
(978) 544-3696, Fax: (978) 544-8271

Pacific Glass Auctions
1507 21st Street, Suite #203
Sacramento, CA 95814
(800) 806-7722, Fax: (916) 443-3199
info@pacglass.com
www.pacglass.com

Howard B. Parzow, Auctioneers
(Advertising)
P.O. Box 3464
Gaithersburg, MD 20885-3464
(301) 977-6741

Past Tyme Pleasures
(925) 484-6442
pasttyme@excite.com

Pettigrew Antique & Collector Auctions,
Division of R. G. Cannon Attractions
P.O. Box 38159
Colorado Springs, CO 80937-8159
(719) 633-7963, Fax: (719) 633-5035

Phillips Fine Arts & Auctioneers,
Alexandra Peters
(Movie Memorabilia)
406 East 79th Street
New York, NY 10022
(212) 570-4830

Phillips International
Auctioneers & Valuers
406 East 79th Street
New York, NY 10021
(212) 570-4830, Fax: (212) 570-2207
www.phillips-auctions.com

Playle's Online Auctions, Ron Playle
(Stamps/Postcards)
P.O. Box 65918
West Des Moines, IA 50265
(515) 267-1490

The Political Gallery, Tom Slater
5335 North Takoma Avenue
Indianapolis, IN 46220
(317) 257-0863

Postcards International
2321 Whitney Avenue, Suite 102
P.O. Box 5398
Hamden, CT 06518
(203) 248-6621
www.csmonline.com/post-cardsint

Poster Auctions International,
Terry Shargel
(Posters)
601 West 26th Street
New York, NY 10001
(212) 787-4000
www.posterauction.com

Rasdale Stamp Company
36 South Street, Suite 1102
Chicago, IL 60630
(312) 263-7334

Paul A. Riseman
(Sheet Music)
2205 South Park Avenue
Springfield, IL 62704-4335
(217) 787-2634

Steve Ritter Auctioneering
34314 West 120th Street
Excelsior Springs, MO 64024
(816) 833-2855

Sandy Rosnick Auctions
15 Front Street
Salem, MA 01970
(508) 741-1130

Jacques C. Schiff, Jr., Inc.
(Stamps)
195 Main Street
Ridgefield Park, NJ 07660-1620
(201) 641-5566

Shute Auction Gallery, Philip C. Shute
(Art/Antiques)
850 West Chestnut Street
Brockton, MA 02401
(508) 588-0022

Robert A. Siegel Auction Galleries
65 East 55th Street
New York, NY 10022
(212) 753-6421

Skinner, Inc.
(Art/Antiques)
63 Park Plaza
Boston, MA 02116
(617) 350-5400, Fax: (617) 350-5429
info@skinnerinc.com
www.skinnerinc.com

Slotin Folk Art Auctions, Steve Slotin
(Folk Art)
5967 Blackberry Lane
Buford, GA 30518
(770) 932-1000

Sotheby's
(Art/Antiques)
1334 York Avenue
New York, NY 10021
(212) 606-7000

Stamp Auction Central, Thomas Droege
20 West Colony, Suite 120
Durham, NC 27705
(919) 403-9459

Stamps for Collectors, Dennis Abel
(651) 639-3957
www.drabel.com

Steffen's Historical Militaria,
Roger S. Steffen
(Historical Items)
14 Murnan Road
Cold Springs, KY 41076-9723
(859) 431-4499

Stuckey Auction Company
315 West Broad Street
Richmond, VA 23225
(804) 780-0850

Southern Folk Pottery Collectors Society
220 Washington Street
Bennett, NC 27208
(336) 581-4246

Superior Galleries
9478 West Olympic Boulevard
Beverly Hills, CA 90212
(310) 203-9855

Swann Galleries, Caroline Birenbaum
(Posters/Art on Paper)
104 East 25th Street
New York, NY 10010
(212) 254-4710

Treadway Galleries
2029 Madison Road
Cincinnati, OH 45208
(513) 321-6742
www.a3c2net.com/tread-waygallery

Victorian Images
Box 284
Marlton, NJ 08053
(856) 354-2154, Fax: (856) 354-9699
rmascieri@aol.com
www.tradecards.com/vi

Virginia Postcard Mail Auction,
John H. McClintock
P.O. Box 1765
Manassas, VA 20108
(703) 368-2757

Weschler's, Nicole Arnn
909 East Street N.W.
Washington, DC 20004
(202) 628-1281

York Town Auctions, John McClain
(Folk Art/Antiques)
1625 Haviland Road
York, PA 17404
(717) 751-0211

Young Fine Arts Auctions,
George M. Young
P.O. Box 313
North Berwick, ME 03906
(207) 676-3104

Other Resources

Books

Alsford, Denis. *Match Holder: 100 Years of Ingenuity.* Schiffer Publishing, 1994.

Ames, Kenneth L. *Beyond Necessity: Art in the Folk Tradition.* The Winterthur Museum, 1977.

Astolat, John. *Phillimore: The Postcard Art of R. P. Phillimore.* London: Greenfriar Press, 1985.

Ayers, James. *Pepsi-Cola Bottles Collectors Guide.* Mount Airy, NC: R. J. Menter Enterprises, 1998.

Banneck, Janet A. *Antique Postcards of Rose O'Neill.* Greater Chicago Productions, 1992.

Barlow, Ron and Ray Reynolds. *Insider's Guide to Old Books, Magazines, Newspapers, and Trade Catalogs.* Windmill Publishing, 1996.

Barnicoat, John. *A Concise History of Posters, 1870-1970.* Harry N. Abrams, Inc., 1972.

Bernhard, Willi. *Picture Postcard Catalogue, 1870-1945.* Hamburg: Willi Bernhard, 1972.

Bishop, Robert. *American Folk Sculpture.* E. P. Dutton & Co., Inc., 1974.

Black, Mary and Jean Lipman. *American Folk Painting.* Clarkson N. Potter, Inc., 1966.

Buday, George. *The History of the Christmas Card.* Spring Books, 1954.

Burdick, J. R. *Pioneer Postcards.* Franklin Square, NY: Nostalgia Press, 1957.

Carline, Richard. *Pictures in the Post.* Deltiologists of America, 1971.

Chase, Ernest Dudley. *The Romance of Greeting Cards.* Tower Books, 1971.

Collins, Herbert. *Threads of History.* Smithsonian Institution Press, 1979.

Cross, K. W. *Charlton Price Guide to First World War Canadian Infantry Badges.* The Charlton Press, 1995.

Czulewicz, Gerald E., Sr. *The Foremost Guide to Uncle Sam Collectibles.* Collector Books, 1995.

DeWitt, J. Doyle. *A Century of Campaign Buttons. 1789-1889,* Travelers Press, 1959.

Dillon, Debbie. *Collectors Guide to Sheet Music.* L-W Promotions, 1988.

Dyer, Rod, Jim Heimann, and H. Thomas Steele. *Close Cover Before Striking.* Abbeville Press, 1987.

Eatwell, John M. and David K. Clint III. *Pike's Peak Gold.* Denver, CO: self-published, 2345 South Federal Boulevard, Suite 100, Denver, CO 80219.

Edmundson, Barbara. *Historical Shot Glasses.* Chico, CA: self-published, 1995.

The Encyclopedia of Collectibles: Folk Art to Horse Drawn Carriages. Alexandria, VA: Time-Life Books, 1978.

The Encyclopedia of Collectibles: Phonographs to Quilts. Alexandria, VA: Time-Life Books, 1979.

Fanelli, Gioanni and Ezio Godoli. *Art Nouveau Postcards.* New York: Rizzoli International Publications, 1987.

Fielding, Mantle. *Dictionary of American Painters, Sculptors and Engravers.* Green Farms, CT: Modern Books and Crafts, Inc., 1926, 1974.

Folk Art in America: A Living Tradition. The High Museum of Art, 1974.

Gallo, Max. *The Poster in History.* American Heritage Publishing Company, 1974.

Gutzman, W. L. *The Canadian Patriotic Post Card Handbook: 1900-1914.* Toronto: Unitrade Press, 1985.

Gutzman, W. L. *The Canadian Picture Post Card Catalogue 1988.* Toronto: Unitrade Press, 1987.

Hake, Theodore L. *Encyclopedia of Political Buttons, Book II, 1920-1976.* Americana & Collectibles Press, 1977.

Hake, Theodore L. *Encyclopedia of Political Buttons, Book III, 1789-1916.* Americana & Collectibles Press, 1978.

Hake, Theodore L. *Encyclopedia of Political Buttons, United States, 1896-1972.* Americana & Collectibles Press, 1985.

Hake, Theodore L. *Hake's Guide to Presidential Campaign Collectibles.* Wallace-Homestead, 1992.

Hastin, Bud. *Avon Products & California Perfume Co., Collector's Encyclopedia 16th Edition 2001.* Kansas City, MO: Bud Hastin's Publications, 2001.

Hemphill, Herbert W., Jr. *Folk Sculpture USA.* The Brooklyn Museum, 1976.

Hemphill, Herbert W., Jr. and Julia Weissman. *Twentieth-Century American Art and Artists.* E. P. Dutton & Company Inc., 1974.

Hershenson, Bruce and Richard Allen. *War Movie Posters.* published by Bruce Hershenson, P.O. Box 874, West Plains, MO 65775, 2000.

Hill, C. W. *Discovering Picture Postcards.* Aylesbury, England: Shire Publications Ltd., 1970.

Hinrichs, Kit and Delphine Hirasuna. *Long May She Wave: A Graphic History of the American Flag.* Ten Speed Press, 2001.

Holt, Tonie and Valmai Holt. *I'll Be Seeing You: Picture Postcards of World War II.* England: Moorland Publishing Company, 1987.

Holt, Tonie and Valmai Holt. *Picture Postcards of the Golden Age.* London: Postcard Publishing Company, 1978.

Holt, Tonie and Valmai Holt. *Till the Boys Come Home.* Ridley Park, PA: Deltiologists of America, 1978.

Hornung, Clarence P. *Treasury of American Design.* 2 vols. Harry N. Abrams, Inc., 1972.

Horwitz, Elinor Lander. *The Bird, the Banner and Uncle Sam: Images of America in Folk and Popular Art.* Philadelphia, PA and New York: J. B. Lippincott Company, 1976.

Huxford, Bob and Sharon Huxford. *Huxford's Collectible Advertising.* 4th ed. Collector Books, 1999.

Jacobs, Martin. *World War II Homefront Collectibles, Price & Identification Guide.* Krause Publications, 2000.

Johnson, Don and Elizabeth Johnson. *Warman's Advertising.* Krause Publications, 2000.

Kernall, Juli. *Postcard Collector 1999 Annual & Price Guide.* 8th ed. Antique Trader Books, 1998.

Klug, Ray. *Antique Advertising Encyclopedia,* vol. 1 (1978, 1993 update), vol. 2 (1985, 1990 update), L-W Book Sales

Kurella, Elizabeth. *The Complete Guide to Vintage Textiles.* Krause Publications, 1999.

Lipman, Jean. *American Folk Art in Wood, Metal and Stone.* Dover Publications, Inc., 1972.

Lipman, Jean. *American Primitive Painting.* Dover Publications, Inc., 1969.

Lipman, Jean and Alice Winchester. *The Flowering of American Folk Art: 1776-1876.* The Viking Press, 1974.

Lund, Brian. *Postcard Collecting: A Beginner's Guide.* Nottingham, England: Reflections of a Bygone Age, 1985.

Manchester, Herbert. *The Diamond Match Company: A Century of Service, of Progress, and of Growth: 1835-1935.* New York: Diamond Match Company, 1935.

Marx, Roger. *Masters of the Poster, 1896-1900.* Images Graphiques, 1977.

Mashburn, J. L. *Artist-Signed Postcard Price Guide.* Colonial House, 1993.

Mashburn, J. L. *Black Americana Postcard Price Guide,* 2nd ed. Colonial House, 1996.

Mashburn, J. L. *Postcard Price Guide,* 4th ed. Colonial House, 2001.

Mastai, Boleslaw and Marie-Louise D'Otrange Mastai. *The Stars and the Stripes: The American Flag as Art and as History from the Birth of the Republic to the Present.* New York: Alfred A. Knopf, 1973.

Matthew, Jack. *Toys Go to War: World War II Military Toys, Games, Puzzles & Books.* Pictorial Histories Publishing, 1994.

McKearin, Helen and George S. McKearin. *American Glass.* New York: Crown Publishers, 1956.

McKearin, Helen and George S. McKearin. *Two Hundred Years of American Blown Glass.* New York: Crown Publishers, 1950.

McKearin, Helen and Kenneth M. Wilson. *American Bottles and Flasks and Their Ancestry.* New York: Crown Publishers, 1978.

Megson, Frederic and Mary Megson. *American Advertising Postcards.* self-published, 1985.

Menchine, Ron. *Propaganda Postcards of World War II.* Krause Publications, 2000.

Milgram, James W. *Presidential Campaign Illustrated Envelopes and Letter Paper 1840-1972.* David G. Phillips Publishing Company, Inc., 33161

Miller, George and Dorothy Miller. *Picture Postcards in the United States 1893-1918.* Clarkson N. Potter, Inc., 1976.

Mott, Frank Luther. *A History of American Magazines.* Cambridge, MA: The Belknap Press of Harvard University Press, 1957.

Nicholson, Susan Brown. *Antique Post Card Sets and Series Price Guide.* Greater Chicago Publications, 1993.

Nicholson, Susan Brown. *Encyclopedia of Antique Postcards.* Wallace-Homestead, 1994.

Nicholson, Susan Brown. *Postcard Collector Annual,* 6th ed. Antique Trader Books, 1996.

Odell, John. *Indian Bottles & Brands, Lebanon, Ohio.* Odell Publishing, 1998.

Pafik, Marie-Reine A. and Anna Marie Guiheen. *The Sheet Music Reference & Price Guide,* 2nd ed. Collector Books, 1995 (Values Updated 2000).

Perkins, Edgar. *Matchcover: The World's Most Fascinating Hobby.* Washington, DC, 1956.

Petretti, Alan. *Petretti's Soda Pop Collectibles Price Guide,* 1st ed. Dubuque, IA: Antique Trader Books, 2001.

Priest, Daniel B. *American Sheet Music with Prices.* Wallace-Homestead, 1978.

Rancier, Esther. *Matchcovers: A Guide to Collecting.* Watkins Glen, NY: Century House Inc., 1976.

Reed, Walt and Roger Reed. *The Illustrator in America, 1880–1980: A Century of Illustrations.* New York: Madison Square Press, Inc., 1984.

Rendell, Joan. *The Match, the Box and the Label.* London: David & Charles, 1983.

Retskin, Bill. *The Matchcover Collector's Price Guide,* 2nd ed. Antique Trader Books/Krause Publications, 1997.

Robbins, Trina. *930 Matchbook Advertising Cuts of the Twenties and Thirties (Pictorial Archive Series).* Dover Publications, 1997.

Rubin, Cynthia and Morgan Williams. *Larger Than Life: The American Tail-Tale Postcard.* Abbeville Press, 1990.

Ryan, Dorothy. *Picture Postcard in the United States, 1893–1918.* New York: Clarkson Potter, 1982.

Samuels, Peggy and Harold Samuels. *Samuels' Encyclopedia of Artists of the American West.* Castle, Inc., 1985.

Schroeder's Antique Price Guide. Paducah, KY: Collector Books, 2002.

Schroy, Ellen T. *Warman's Americana & Collectibles,* 10th ed. Iola, WI: Krause Publications, 2001.

Schroy, Ellen T. *Warman's Antiques and Collectibles Price Guide,* 36th ed. Iola, WI: Krause Publications, 2002.

Shelley, Donald A. *The Fraktur-Writing or Illuminated Manuscripts of the Pennsylvania Germans.* The Pennsylvania German Folklore Society, 1961.

Short, Marion. *Hollywood Movie Songs: Collectible Sheet Music.* Schiffer Publications, 1999.

Smith, Jack. *Military Postcards.* Lombard, IL: Wallace Homestead, 1988.

Smith, Jack H. *Postcard Companion: The Collector's Reference*. Randor, PA: Wallace-Homestead Book Company, 1989.

Sotheby's *"Important Americana" Auction Catalog: The American Flag Collection of Thomas S. Connelly*. May 23, 2002.

Stadtmiller, Bernard. *Postcard Collecting: A Fun Investment*. Palm Bay, FL: Bernard Stadtmiller, 1973.

Stewart, Nicholas. *James Montgomery Flagg: Uncle Sam and Beyond*. Collector's Press, 1997.

Sullivan, Edmund B. *American Political Badges and Medalets, 1789-1892*. Quarterman Publications, 1981.

Sullivan, Edmund B. *Collecting Political Americana*. Christopher Publishing House, 1991.

Summers, B. J. *Antique & Contemporary Advertising Memorabilia, Identification & Value Guide*. Paducah, KY: Collector Books, 2002.

Sweeney, Rick. *Collecting Applied Color Label Soda Bottles*. La Mesa, CA, 2002.

Tutton, John. *Udderly Delightful*. Stephens City, VA: Commercial Press, Inc., 1996.

United States Postal Service. *The Postal Service Guide to U.S. Stamps*, 28th ed. Harper Collins Publishers, 2001.

Warda, Mark. *Political Campaign Stamps*. Krause Publications, 1998.

Welch, Naomi. *American and European Postcards of Harrison Fisher Illustrator*. Images of the Past, 1999.

Zimmerman, David. *Encyclopedia of Advertising Tins*, vol. 2. Paducah, KY: Collector Books, 1999.

Periodicals

Advertising

Advertising Collectors Express, P.O. Box 221, Mayview, MO 64071

National Association of Paper and Advertising Collectors, P.O. Box 500, Mount Joy, PA 17552-0500, (717) 492-2540

Paper Collectors Marketplace, P.O. Box 128, Scandinavia, WI 54977

Art

American Art Review, 12230 State Line Road, Shawnee Mission, KS 66209, (913) 451-8801

Art & Antiques, 2100 Powers Ferry Road, Atlanta, GA 30339, (770) 955-5656

Art & Auction, 11 East 36th Street, New York, NY 10016, (800) 777-8718

The Art Newspaper, 80 East 11th Street, New York, NY 10003, (212) 475-4574

Art on Paper Journal, 39 East 78th Street, #501, New York, NY 10021-0213, (212) 988-5959

The Fine Arts Trader, P.O. Box 1273, Randolph, MA 02368, (800) 332-5055

Illustrator Collector's News, P.O. Box 1958, Sequim, WA 98392

Morgogen Associates Newsletter, P.O. Box 324, Mountain Lakes, NJ 07046, (973) 334-0675

Bottles

Antique Bottle & Glass Collector, 102 Jefferson Street, P.O. Box 187, East Greenville, PA 18041, (215) 679-5849

Bottles and Extras, 3706 Deerfield Cove, P.O. Box 341062, Bartlett, TN 38135, (901) 372-8428

Folk Art

Folk Art, Columbus Avenue at 66th Street, New York, NY 10023-6214, (212) 977-7298

Folk Art Finder, 1 River Road, Essex, CT 06426, (860) 767-0313

Folk Art Messenger, P.O. Box 17041, Richmond, VA 23226-7041, (804) 285-4532

Magazines

Paper Collectors' Marketplace, P.O. Box 128, Scandinavia, WI 54977

Pulp & Paperback Market Newsletter, 5813 York Avenue, Edina, MN 55410

Matchbook Covers

The Front Striker Bulletin, The American Matchcover Collecting Club,
P.O. Box 18481, Asheville, NC 28814-0481

Liberty Bell Crier, Liberty Bell Matchcover Club, 2501 Maryland Avenue #7,
Willow Grove, PA 19090-1835

Matchcover Beachcomber, Long Beach Matchcover Club, 2501 West Sunflower,
H-5, Santa Ana, CA 92704-7503

Matchcover Classified, 16425 Dam Road #3, Clearlake, CA 95422

Match Hunter, 740 Poplar, Boulder, CO 80304

RMS Bulletin, Rathkamp Matchcover Society, 2659 Eckard Way, Auburn, CA 95603

Windy City Matchcover News, Windy City Matchcover Club,
1307 College Avenue, Apt. 12, Wheaton, IL 60187

Movie Posters and Memorabilia

American Movie Classics Magazine, P.O. Box 469082, Marion, OH 46908,
(888) 262-4700

Big Reel Magazine, P.O. Box 1050, Dubuque, IA 52004, (800) 334-7165

Classic Images Newspaper, 301 East Third Street, Muscatine, IA 52761, (319) 263-2331

Films of the Golden Age Magazine, 301 East Third Street, Muscatine, IA 52761,
(319) 263-2331

Movie Collector's World, P.O. Box 309, Fraser, MI 48026, (810) 774-4311

Movie Poster Price Almanac, P.O. Box 114, Hyde Park, NY 12538-0114, (845) 452-1998

Movie Poster Update, 2401 Broad Street, Chattanooga, TN 37408

Paper Collectors Marketplace Magazine, 470 Main Street, Scandinavia, WI 54977,
(715) 467-2379

Past Times Nostalgia Network Newsletter, 7308 H Filmore Drive, Buena Park,
CA 90620, (714) 527-5845

Political Items

The Political Bandwagon, P.O. Box 348, Leola, PA 17540-0348, (717) 656-7855

The Political Collector Newspaper, P.O. Box 5171, York, PA 17405-5171, (717) 846-0418

Postcards

Barr's Post Card News, 70 South Sixth Street, Lansing, IA 52151-9680, (319) 538-4500

Gloria's Corner, P.O. Box 507, Denison, TX 75021-0507, (903) 463-4878

Postcard Collector, P.O. Box 1050, Dubuque, IA 52004-1050, (800) 334-7165

Sheet Music

The Rag Times, 15522 Ricky Court, Grass Valley, CA 95949-6672

Sheet Music Magazine, 333 Adams Street, Bedford Hills, NY 10507, (800) 759-3036

Stamps

Global Stamp News, P.O. Box 97, Sidney, OH 45365-0097, (937) 492-3183

Linn's Stamp News, P.O. Box 29, Sidney, OH 45365, (937) 498-0801

Mekeel's & Stamps Magazine, P.O. Box 5050, White Plains, NY 10602, (800) 635-3351

Philatelic Focus Newsletter, 501 Fifth Avenue, Suite 1901, New York, NY 10017-6017, (212) 867-3699

Scott's Stamp Monthly, P.O. Box 828, Sidney, OH 45365-0828, (937) 498-0802

Stamp Collector, 700 East State Street, Iola, WI 54990-0001, (715) 445-2214

USA Philatelic, Information Fulfillment, Department 6270, U.S. Postal Service, P.O. Box 219014, Kansas City, MO 64121

U.S. Stamp News, P.O. Box 5050, White Plains, NY 10602, (800) 635-3351

World Wars I and II

American Militaria Sourcebook & Directory, 741 Miller Drive S.E., Suite D-2, Leesburg, VA 20175, (703) 779-8318

Journal of the War of 1812 & the Era 1880-1840, 844 East Pratt Street, Baltimore, MD 21202, (410) 223-1638

Military Collector News, P.O. Box 702073, Tulsa, OK 74170

Military History, 6405 Frank Drive, Harrisburg, PA 17112

Military International, P.O. Box 43440, Minneapolis, MN 55443-0400, (888) 428-1942

Military News Magazine, 2122 28th Street, Sacramento, CA 95818, (800) 366-9192

Military Trader, P.O. Box 1050, Dubuque, IA 52004-1050, (800) 334-7165

Index

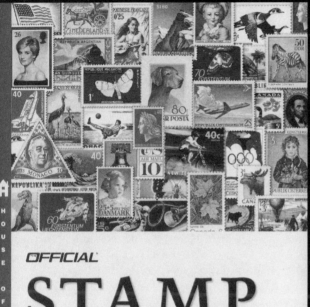

HOUSE OF COLLECTIBLES SERIES

THE OFFICIAL PRICE GUIDES TO

Title	ISBN	Price	Author
Collecting Books, 4th ed.	0609807692	$18.00	Marie Tedford & Pat Goudey
Collector Knives, 13th ed.	0676601898	$17.95	C. Houston Price
Collector Plates, 7th ed.	0676601545	$19.95	Rinker Enterprises
Costume Jewelry, 3rd ed.	0609806688	$17.95	Harrice Simmons Miller
Dinnerware of the 20th Century	0676600859	$29.95	Harry L. Rinker
Glassware, 3rd ed.	067660188X	$17.00	Mark Pickvet
Hake's Character Toys, 4th ed.	0609808222	$35.00	Ted Hake
Hislop's International Fine Art	0609808745	$20.00	Duncan Hislop
Military Collectibles, 6th ed.	0676600522	$20.00	Richard Austin
Mint Errors, 6th ed.	0609808559	$15.00	Alan Herbert
Overstreet Comic Book Grading Guide	0609810529	$24.00	Robert Overstreet & Arnold Blumberg
Overstreet Comic Books, 32nd ed.	0609808214	$22.00	Robert M. Overstreet
Overstreet Indian Arrowheads, 7th ed.	0609808699	$24.00	Robert M. Overstreet
Pottery & Porcelain, 8th ed.	0876378939	$18.00	Harvey Duke
Records, 16th ed.	0609809083	$25.95	Jerry Osborne
Silverware of the 20th Century	0676600867	$24.95	Harry L. Rinker
Stemware of the 20th Century	0676600840	$24.95	Harry L. Rinker
Vintage Fashion and Fabrics	0609808133	$17.00	Pamela Smith

THE OFFICIAL GUIDES TO

Title	ISBN	Price	Author
America's State Quarters	0609807706	$5.99	David L. Ganz
Flea Market Prices	0609807722	$14.95	Harry L. Rinker
How to Make Money in Coins Right Now, 2nd ed.	0609807463	$14.95	Scott Travers
One-Minute Coin Expert, 4th ed.	0609807471	$7.99	Scott Travers
Stamp Collector's Bible	0609808842	$22.00	Stephen R. Datz
U.S. Flea Markets, 8th ed.	0609809229	$14.00	Kitty Werner

THE OFFICIAL BECKETT SPORTS CARDS PRICE GUIDES TO

Title	ISBN	Price	Author
Baseball Cards 2003, 23rd ed.	06099810375	$7.99	Dr. James Beckett
Basketball Cards 2003, 12th ed.	0609809849	$7.99	Dr. James Beckett
Football Cards 2003, 22nd ed.	0609809857	$7.99	Dr. James Beckett

THE OFFICIAL BLACKBOOK PRICE GUIDES TO

Title	ISBN	Price	Author
U.S. Coins 2003, 41st ed.	067660174X	$7.99	Marc & Tom Hudgeons
U.S. Paper Money 2003, 35th ed.	0609809482	$6.99	Marc & Tom Hudgeons
U.S. Postage Stamps 2003, 25th ed.	0609809490	$8.99	Marc & Tom Hudgeons
World Coins 2003, 6th ed.	0676601774	$7.99	Marc & Tom Hudgeons

Available in bookstores everywhere!